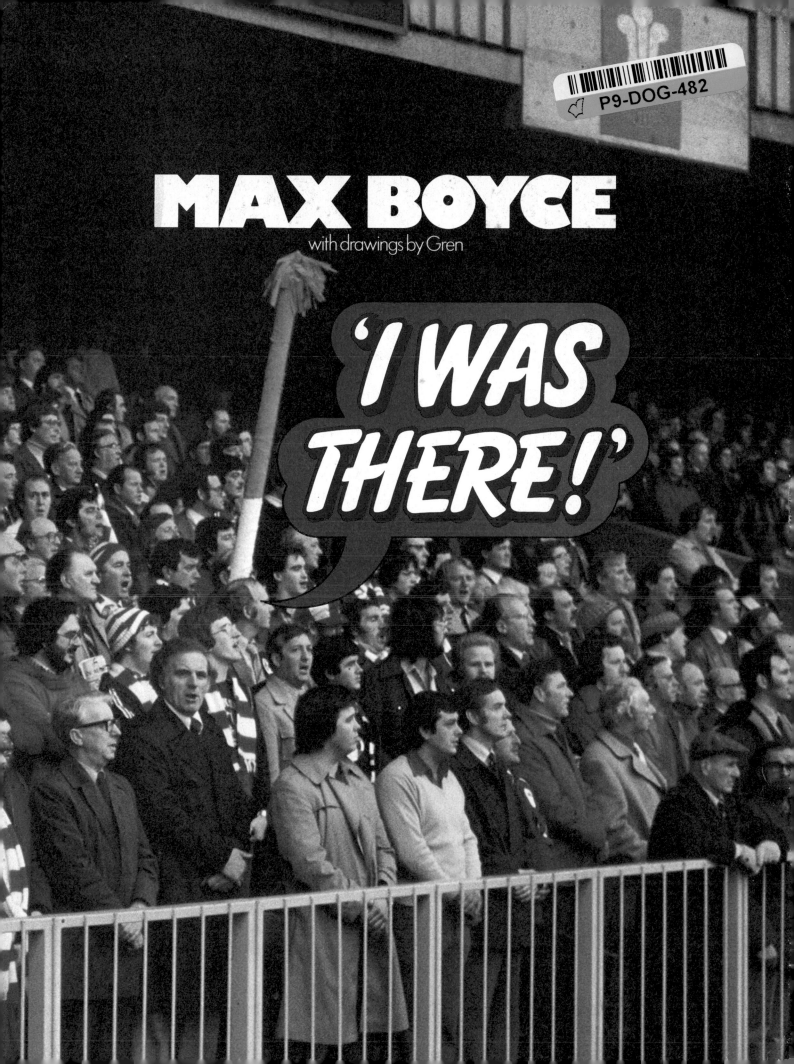

MAX BOYCE

with drawings by Gren

'I WAS THERE!'

CONTENTS

© Max Boyce 1979

All rights reserved.

Designed by Bernard Higton for
George Weidenfeld and Nicolson Ltd
91 Clapham High Street, London SW4

Special photography by Michael Busselle.

Other photographs supplied by
Max Boyce 9, 49, 68/69; Colorsport 30, 32, 36 (bottom right),
43, 44; Craely's Studios, Cardiff 2/3, 18 (top left); EMI 12;
Christine Goode, Glynneath 89; Robert Alwyn Hughes 18/19;
Keystone 6/7, 81 (top right); B. Mitchell 4/5, 21;
Picturepoint, London 92; S&G Press/Agency 21 (top);
Wales Tourist Board 80; Bamforth Marketing 93

Calligraphy (46) by Freda Harmer
Drawing (73) by Cathy

Press cuttings reproduced by kind permission of
The Llanelli Star and The Western Mail

The publishers acknowledge permission to use material of the
following copyright holders:
Ambleside Music Ltd: pages 20, 22, 40, 45, 73, 94.
Land of Song Music Ltd: pages 17, 27, 29, 38, 43, 48, 51, 59, 61,
66, 70, 74, 84.
Maxbo Music Ltd: pages 13, 19, 24, 33, 46, 47, 52, 56, 60, 62, 65,
68, 76, 78, 83, 86, 89, 90, 92.
St Anne's Music Ltd: pages 14, 30, 34, 81.

ISBN 0 297 77609 6

Printed in Great Britain by Redwood Burn Ltd
Trowbridge & Esher.

DEDICATION

To my mother, Jean and Cathy, and
The Rev Goronwy Roberts
Dyfnallt Morgan
Harry Morgan's grannie
Will
The Penygraig R.F.C. groundstaff
P.N.V.C.C.
Felinfoel Brewery
John Davies, and Billy Jewel for the songs
President Amin
Mary Whitehouse
Steve Mostyn Evans
Dr Peregrine Cleggs
Harry Dampers and all at the Outside-Half factory
Bill Clement and the W.R.U.
Frank Bough and 'Grandstand'
John the Baptist
The Devil
Anne (Crumlin)
All at Pontypool Conservative Club
Ty-Nant farm
Brian Lewis for all his help and for S.T.G.1.S.
Mel Thomas
Idris and all at Bastille Louis XV
Rudyard Kipling
Brynmawr and Maesteg R.F.C.
Madame Tussaud
Russ 'I'm in charge' Stanley
Ashes
The R.F.U.
The Rediffusion man
Madame Clara Teifi Jenkins D.Mus(E) L.R.A.M.
  F.R.C.M. Ph.D.(Oxon)
Ivor Morgan and Ivor Emmanuel
Sergeant Davies and Idris Walters (Bridgend)
L.T. Lloyd J.P. and Hughie . . .
The Rev. Prydderch Pugh and Matt Bucklou
Morgan the Moon and all at Mission Control
The Sunshine Home (Dublin)
All at the 'Hope and Anchor'
Mrs Davies (ART)
All at 'Shangrila'
The St. Alban's Brass Band
Harrie Thomas

Will 'McGonagle' Morgan
Jonathan Lever for being eighty seven per cent behind me
Griff Fenders Vans
Davies the Vet
The Queen
Prince Charles
Dai Tolerance and all at F.23
The late Brian Harries and the Valley folk
  club Pontardawe
The 'walking dead' and all at the bakery in Hawick
Stan the Pies
Maggie
Alun (Scruggs) Chesterfield
Berni Inns, H.P. brown sauce and Anjou Rosé
Y Wiwer
Dewi Griffiths (BBC)
The late Derek Boote, the Triban and Alun 'What I
  like about this boy' Williams
Julia
Edward (am ddeall)
The Rev. Elwyn Davies (Trebanos) am 'Ar goll'
  ar lleill
Rene 'It's in the post' Taylor
Keith 'It was 110° in the Waterbag' Jones,
  John Howard, Joe Lord, Russell Perry, Stuart,
  Ken Grayling, Griff 'We've sold the balcony' Hunt,
  Roy Bowden (N.Z.)
Gareth Owen for 'Llanbaglan'
Bob Barrett and all at EMI (M.O.R.)
David Norrie (Womens Realm, Rugby World and Scotland)
Neil Lewis for his invaluable contribution and
  for his 'performance' at Otley Rugby Club . . .
  'I fell in love when love was blind . . .'
John Luce for his reliability and professionalism —
  and for finding my plectrums
  Rob Allen for saving my life in a Sydney
  Fountain . . . don't go changing
Jack 'Ye of little faith' Williams for not
  doubting me, Margaret (when can we have the
  words) Price — and Tarquin
Jack 'It's like a whelk stall' Edgar
Andrew 'I can handle it' Greenwood
My faithful roadies
Tom 'Ricky Ticky Tick' Reid and the Trades —
  for many a wee dram and a song
Bert and Minnie for the partin' gift o' heather
Margaret for 'Ar lan y môr'
Lott Darryl and 'A' Shift
Colin 'It's all looking very good' Webb for
  the opportunity
Gerald Davies, Gareth, Phill, John, Terry and Barry
  for the memories
Clever Trevor for a little bit of yesteryear
The County Hotel Taunton for reseeding the lawn
  after the International
Ieuan Lewis (Pontardawe) for all his help in the early days
Big Bob, Sandy and the 'Cod Gutters' . . . I'd
  rather have a paper doll
The Crowd at Cardiff Arms Park for 'Hymns
  and Arias'
Billy 'I'm all over the back page' Jenkins and
  Terry Williams J.P.
Vince Goode for looking after my 'beans' when
  I was in Australia
And last but not least Stuart Littlewood for all he's done

8

INTRODUCTION

In the window of 'Harries the Papershop' — the Square, Glynneath, was displayed a postcard which read: 'Guitar For Sale — Four pounds (or nearest offer). Apply: 164, Morfa Glâs, Glynneath'.

I called at the address and, pretending to know everything that there was to know about guitars, proceeded to examine the fretboard and to ascertain whether or not the neck was warped (not that I would have known if it was). Then, with a few well timed grimaces and suitable frowns, I convinced the owner that I was a leading authority on the folk-guitar and eventually, after a few more frowns, we agreed on a price of three pounds, ten shillings.

Even then my mother considered it a waste of money, and that eventually it would suffer the same fate as my butterfly and stamp collections. However it was not to be and, armed with my *Bert Weedon Play in a Day Guitar Guide*, I subjected my mother and my grandfather to almost continuous tortured attempts at 'Little Brown Jug' and 'Cockles and Mussels'.

I remember the first great problem I encountered was the chord of 'F'. This is how it was illustrated in a book I bought at the time called *2001 Chords for the Guitar*.

Each dot on the diagram represents a finger position on the fretboard of the guitar. I was convinced in those early days that the author of the book was completely mad and that it was absolutely impossible to play the chord of 'F' (all it entails is using the thumb to press down the sixth string and the first finger to press down *both* the first and second strings). I thought then however, that you needed a deformity of the left hand in order to achieve it.

Despite my doubts I persevered and with the aid of some plastic surgery I played my first 'F'. Even when I was younger I had not been gifted with a great deal of musical ability. It was true I had received the top mark in music during my first year at school but it

My first attempt at song writing took the form of humorous verse (in 'talking Blues' fashion), involving my friends at the cricket club. With their many local references, these early offerings could only appeal to those directly concerned and made little sense to those outside my own circle of friends.

Nevertheless, I had experienced for the first time the thrill of making people laugh with words and music that I had written. Fired then with enthusiasm, I began writing verse and songs that, hopefully, everyone could understand, but that still reflected life in the type of community in which I was born — South Wales. It was that close-knit community with its inherent warmth and humour, its sadness and its passion, that was to be, undoubtedly, my greatest influence. I attempted to write songs that ordinary people could identify with and recognise a thread of truth in my words.

was only because I could draw violins better than anyone else. However, I gradually improved until I was able to play adequately.

It was not always easy to find a willing ear for my songs and stories, so I will always be grateful to the Valley Folk Club in Pontardawe, with its inspired chorus singing and intimate friendly atmosphere, for their encouragement and enthusiasm, but most of all for listening. It was they who consciously and unconsciously stimulated me to create song.

This book therefore is an illustrated collection of my songs, stories and poems.

If through my words and music others can enjoy sharing my experiences, then my songs were worth singing, my stories worth telling . . . and this book worth writing!

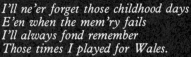

I'll ne'er forget those childhood days
E'en when the mem'ry fails
I'll always fond remember
Those times I played for Wales.

In the mining valleys in which I was brought up everybody has played for Wales, few however have actually pulled on the scarlet jersey and run onto Cardiff Arms Park, but we've all played at some time or other.

We had our own 'national stadiums' in streets and in backlanes and on bits of waste ground behind welfare halls, where rubbish bins became goalposts and tin sheets became corner flags.

They were multi-purpose grounds for in the summer they became 'The Oval' and 'Lords' and other famous test-cricket grounds. The 'goalposts' became wickets, the tin sheets became the sightscreens and Clive Davies' father's garage became the Pavilion end.

One of my friends, Owen Phillips, was the finest 'street' opening bat I have ever seen. He used to draw the wickets with white chalk on the back door of his house. When you claimed you'd 'bowled' him he'd deny it saying 'There's no chalk on the ball!' I'd never argue (he was bigger than me) with the result that before the 'out in gardens' rule was introduced he was 'in' once for fourteen weeks. I forget how much he scored, but I know we lost . . .

But it was Rugby we played most . . .

I'll ne'er forget those childhood days
E'en when the mem'ry fails
I'll always fond remember
Those times I played for Wales.

I'll always remember the first time I played for Wales — it was in Llywellyn Street, I was nine at the time and it was against England (it was always against England). I remember we had twenty-eight on our side and . . . three on their side. It wasn't fair but it was my ball!

I remember we won 406-12 in one of those games where you played four hours each way and only stopped when a ball went under a lorry. In that game I scored twenty-three tries before I was carried off injured: I was late tackled into touch three yards short of my anorak.

We went on to beat Ireland and Scotland — before three o'clock. We would have beaten France as well but Mel Thomas kicked the ball into Mrs Harries' garden and she wouldn't let us have it back. She was a funny woman (from Cardiff). We had her back though — we woke her tortoise up and gave it to this drunk and told him it was a pastie.

So then I'd run home and play in the back lane behind my house. I used to make rugby posts out of old kidney-bean sticks; for a ball I used to use an old 'Fairy Liquid' bottle. I was the best kicker of a 'Fairy Liquid' bottle in all Glamorgan. I could screw kick to touch and make the top come off. On thinking back, in all those times never once did we lose. We nearly did once: we were losing to England 36-3 with two minutes to go when — lucky — my mother called me for dinner.

THE INCREDIBLE PLAN

Anyone who has tried to get a ticket for a Rugby International at Cardiff knows how difficult it is.
My Uncle Will, however, got into the ground without a ticket dressed as one of the St Alban's Band (the band that play at Cardiff Arms Park prior to the Internationals).
The trouble was all Will's friends and family got to hear of it ('cos he told Florrie Thomas not to tell anybody) and when the next International was due to be played at Cardiff they all wanted to go as well.

'The Incredible Plan' is the story of what happened.

There's a story that's told in the Valleys
And I'll tell it as best as I can
The story of one Will 'McGonagle' Morgan
And of his 'Incredible Plan'.
It all started off on a cold winter's night
A night that was strangely so still
When the Rugby Club's General Committee
Banned 'Sine Die' their ticket Sec, my Uncle Will
(Mind you, he was in the wrong, we knew all along)
There was no point in petitions or pickets
He was caught with this woman at the back of the stand
With the Club's allocation of tickets.

And what made it worse, she wasn't the first
He'd been caught with Ben Walters' wife Ethel
We all knew her with her fox and her fur
She used to wear on Sundays to Bethel.
Anyway, Will was banned 'Sine Die' — he broke down
    and cried.
I've never seen a man in such sorrow
'Cos like Judas of old he'd sold more than gold
With the Scotland and Wales game tomorrow.
Then he had this idea: he'd go in disguise.
He had it all drawn up and planned
And he went to the game (to his family's shame)
As one of the St Alban's Band.
Back in the village they all got to know
'Make one for me' they'd all say
There was such a demand, it got a bit out of hand
He was making about fifty a day.
So he put an ad, in the *Guardian*
To employ a few men starting Monday
And he did, he started some men — I think about ten,
On three shifts, and some working Sunday.

They made about three or four hundred
When the night shift were sent two till ten.
The jigs were all changed, the tools rearranged,
And they started on ambulance men!
Then they ran out of buttons and bandage —
And policemen were next on the plans.
Whilst 'B' Shift made refs with dark glasses,
Alsatians, white sticks and tin cans!
Then production was brought to a standstill
And the Union could quite understand
When management tabled the motion:
'Things are getting a bit out of hand'.
I'll never forget the day of the match,
The likes of I'll ne'er see again.
I can see them all still coming over the hill:
Hundreds and thousands of men!
The refs came in four double-deckers;
It was going exactly to plan.
And the St Alban's Band came in lorries
And the police in a Griff Fender van!
No I'll never forget that day of the match,

The likes of I'll ne'er see again,
When Queen Street was full of alsatians
And the pubs full of ambulance men!
It was then I saw Will for the first time:
I was standing on the steps by the 'Grand'.
He was in a camel-hair coat (dressed up as a goat)
Marching in front of the Band!
It was then that the accident happened —
The roads were all slippy and wet.
He was knocked down by a man in a greengrocer's van
And they took him to 'Davies the Vet'.
Now 'Davies the Vet' is a bit short-sighted:
He said 'I'm afraid it's his heart.
But he wouldn't have lived longer, even if he'd been stronger:
His eyes are too far apart!'
The funeral was held on a Monday
(The biggest I'd ever seen).
The wreaths came in four double-deckers,
And there was one from Prince Charles and the Queen.
(Sorry, from the 'Prince of Wales' and the 'Queens'!)

There were sprays from three thousand policemen,
And one from the St Alban's Band.
And the bearers were refs with alsatians,
Dark glasses, white sticks and tin cans.
We sang at the graveside the old funeral hymns,
And we all went to comfort his son.
What made him sad, he said, was that 'Dad
Had died not knowing we'd won!'
I couldn't sleep for most of that night,
I kept thinking of what he had said:
'Dad had died not knowing we'd won',
So I dressed when I got out of bed.
And I walked again to that hillside
To that last resting place on a hill.
It was all quiet save when I leant over the grave
And I shouted 'We hammered them Will!!!'
And that story is told in the valleys;
I've told it as best as I can.
The legend of one William 'McGonagle' Morgan,
And of his *Incredible Plan!*

I GAVE MY LOVE A DEBENTURE

Some years ago a debenture scheme was introduced by the Welsh Rugby Union. It took the form of tickets put on sale to help raise money for ground improvements at Cardiff Arms Park.

These tickets or debentures as they are known guarantee the owner the same seat in the stand for all Internationals at Cardiff. They were initially sold at the reasonable price of fifty pounds but have since escalated terrifically in value, eight thousand five hundred pounds having been offered recently for four.

Their present worth however is perhaps best illustrated by the song 'I Gave My Love a Debenture'.

I met her in the Con. Club in Pontypool;
The public bar was crowded so I offered her my stool.
I said 'Fair lass, pray tarry. Come stay awhile with me.
And I'll give you my debenture — Block A, Row 3.'

Her eyes were pale as lyder; her hair was long and black.
The only thing that spoiled her was she wore a plastic mac.
I said 'Fair lass, pray tarry. Come sit upon my knee.'
She thought awhile and then she smiled. I thought
'Ho, ho, he, he, hee hee hee!'

She said she came from Crumlin and that her name
  was Ann.
She told me 'You can walk me home.' I said 'I've got a van!'
We turned into a lay-by, where she told me she loved me.
So I gave her my debenture — Block A, Row 3.

That night I met her mother. (She was waiting for us there.)
Stockings round her ankles and curlers in her hair.
She was waiting on the doorstep, and she waved her fist
  at me.
So I showed her my debenture — Block A, Row 3.

That night when I was sleeping my love proved false to me;
And left me for another who's known as J.B.G.
I know I'll not forget her for she was the rue of me;
And she's got my debenture — Block A, Row 3.

So take my warning all you lads, for girls the likes of she.
They only want you for one thing — your debenture in
  Row 3!
So should you go to Crumlin, pray tread the night with care:
Take heed I pray and stay away from that girl with
  the long black hair.

Above, the old — below, the new

THE NORTH ENCLOSURE SONG

I have always thought it a shame that the North Enclosure was done away with at Cardiff Arms Park. Traditionally it was where the singing always started in International matches. It was there that the greatest 'hwyl'* and atmosphere were always to be found. However, for financial reasons and because of the need for greater crowd control, plastic bucket seating has been installed where for years we had stood in all weathers lashed by wind and rain:

There were times I couldn't see
But it was the only place to be . . .

Oh! I'll sing a fond farewell, and a story I will tell
Of when with my little North Enclosure I was there
And I think it's such a shame, it'll never be the same
As when with my little North Enclosure — I was there

CHORUS
I was there
I was there
With my little North Enclosure I was there

There are stories I can tell, of when I didn't feel too well
But with my little North Enclosure I was there
When there was nowhere I could go and I couldn't wait
  no more
But with my little North Enclosure I was there

Oh I've stood out in the rain and I'd do it all again
With my little North Enclosure I was there
It was there I learnt to sing — 'cos I couldn't see a thing
But with my little North Enclosure I was there

When the ones that had it planned were all sitting in
  the stand
With my little North Enclosure I was there
So I think it's such a shame — it'll never be the same
As when with my little North Enclosure I was there.

* hwyl = fervour, passion, feeling.

I WANDERED LONELY

Any Welsh Rugby supporter who has been without a ticket on the morning of a Welsh Rugby International at Cardiff will understand fully the sentiments expressed in the poem.

I wandered lonely through the crowd
With tired and aching feet.
Ticketless, and down in heart
Where ere I chanced to meet
A man with kindness in his eyes
Who said 'I got a spare'.
I thanked him there down on my knees
And I asked him 'But from where?'

He told me then the saddest tale
Of how his wife and he
Were two debenture holders
(North Stand, Block A, Row D).
But since his wife's dear mother died
Oh, she hasn't been the same
And she doesn't feel like going now.
(And I thought 'What a shame!')

So then I asked 'But why pick on me?
Don't the family want to go?'
He said 'They do, but the kick off's at three
And the funeral's ten to four!'

A tremendous source of humour is to be found in the comments of the 'characters' that frequent the terraces of football matches.

I remember when J.P.R. Williams, the Welsh full back, gathered an awkward rolling ball against Scotland in 1976 and the Scottish wing raced up to tackle him. A Scottish voice shouted from the crowd 'Worry him! Worry him!' A well oiled Welsh voice replied from the bowels of the North Enclosure 'Tell him his mother's ill.'

I'll always remember the first time I went to Dublin to see Wales play Ireland. On the Friday morning we were taken by some friends to visit the Guinness factory. Unfortunately one of the lads who was a bit 'under the weather', slipped on an iron-grilled gangway and fell into a thousand-gallon vat of foaming Guinness and drowned.

On the Saturday morning a BBC Wales news reporter interviewed one of my friends, Billy Williams, who had witnessed the accident. 'Mr Williams, all Wales has been grief-stricken by the sad news of this most unfortunate accident. Can you shed perhaps some small crumb of comfort and tell us, did he suffer? Was it, in fact, a painful death?

'Oh, no!' Billy said, 'he got out three times for a pee!'

THE SCOTTISH TRIP

*Because of the suspicions aroused over the legality of some illnesses our local G.P. has refused doctors' papers during the International Rugby Season. He's now issuing M.O.T. Certificates instead: **M**urrayfield **O**r **T**wickenham. It didn't happen as the song suggests but it could have ... and almost did!*

'The Scottish Trip' was written on a bus going to Scotland on the Tuesday morning for the Scotland/Wales Rugby International when ...

We all had doctors' papers
Not one of us in pain
And Harry Morgan buried
His grannie once again

Oh we went up to the Hielands of Scotland,
To the land of the loch and the glen.
And we'll all bring our wives back a present
So we can go next time again!

CHORUS
Too-ral-ay, oo-ral-ay, addy,
We went up by train and by car.
When the juice of the barley starts flowing
We all saw the game in the bar.

Oh we loaded the bus up with flagons,
And we left about twenty past seven.
We stopped fourteen times between Neath and Bridgend:
We were still in Glamorgan at eleven.

On the M5 Will spoke to the driver,
He said 'Can you no stop this bus for a while?'
He said 'Man alive, we're on the M5.
You'll have to hang on till Carlisle.'

Old Will he climbed out on the sun-roof
And he stood on the bus in disgrace.
He wasn't to know that that bridge was so low,
But he died with a smile on his face!

He was splattered all over the pavement,
And his leek, it was stuffed down his throat.
And I heard his friend say as they scraped Will away
'My ticket was inside his coat!'

When we were up at Edinburgh for the Scotland Wales Rugby International a few years ago we visited Edinburgh Castle on the Saturday morning before the game. Apparently it's the tradition at Edinburgh Castle to fire what they call the 'one o'clock gun', a great cannon which stands on the ramparts of the Castle.
Way down below in Princes Street thousands of red-and-white scarved Welsh Rugby supporters thronged their way through the crowds. One of them however had made his way up to the Castle. I think he was a Neath supporter for he carried a bedraggled banner on which he had written 'Even God is Afraid of Brian Thomas'. As he staggered along, the 'one o'clock gun' was fired. He stopped, blinked and went over to the Scot who had fired the cannon and said 'Take it easy with that cannon pal, there's some of our boys down there!'

WITH A WEE DRAM AND A SONG

'With a Wee Dram and a Song' tells of some of my treasured memories of visiting Scotland for the Scotland/Wales Rugby International at Murrayfield and of the welcome we have always received from the Scottish people. It is because of the affinity, kinship, and friendship we have that:

Some never get to see the game
E'en though we journey long
For they bid us 'Ae Fond Welcome'
With a wee dram and a song.

Oh! We'll go to the highlands of Scotland and to bonnie Teviot dales
And they'll bid us 'ae fond welcome' for we've journeyed far from Wales.
And they'll stand with banners waving in kilt and sporraned throng
And bid us 'ae fond welcome' with a wee dram and a song.

CHORUS
With a wee dram and a song
With a wee dram and a song
They'll bid us ae fond welcome
With a wee dram and a song.

And we'll check into some small hotel and say 'We live by Gâr'
And pay for 'Bed & Breakfast' and never leave the bar
And they'll ask us for a wee Welsh song and your eyes are bloodshot red
And your voice has gone but you carry on — when all you want's your bed.

Then you'll drag yourself to Murrayfield and the snow has turned to rain
And you swear there on the terrace you'll never drink again
And the crowd sing 'Flow'r of Scotland' and you're caught up in the sway
And you spend the first ten minutes facing the other way.

Then it's in some chemist on Sunday, your legs they feel like lead
Asking 'Have you got something for . . .' when you haven't been to bed
Then with bleary eyes we'll all swop ties, and the bus driver says 'c'mon it's
   ten to ten'
And you've gone and squashed your haggis and lost your mac again.

And then you remember . . . you haven't bought a present, and you're wondering
   what to get her
And you're in this M6 Service Station trying to buy a Pringles cashmere sweater
But there's only trains and plastic planes and you're searching all in vain
You've spent four days in Scotland and bought a doll from Spain.

And then it's home on Sunday and another trip it ends
With a parting gift of heather from my 'ain auld border friends'
I'll miss a shift on Monday as aye oft times I've done
Then read the Sunday papers to see if Wales have won.

For some never get to see the game e'en though we journey long
For they bid us 'ae fond welcome with a wee dram and a song'
And if we've lost it matters not for there the sadness ends
For defeat's n'er counted as a loss if it be the gain of friends
And may that friendship ever last and may it journey long
To bid us 'ae fond welcome' with a wee dram and a song!

HYMNS AND ARIAS

'Hymns and Arias' is a song which tells of the trip that thousands of Welshmen make once every two years to see Wales play England at Twickenham.

When it was first sung by the crowd at Cardiff Arms Park someone wrote 'Cwm Rhondda and Calon Lan have found a companion.'

It was undoubtedly one of the greatest moments of my life and it still gives me a great thrill wherever and whenever I hear it sung. I shall always remember that first time . . . I was being interviewed by Frank Bough on 'Grandstand' in front of the North Enclosure at Cardiff Arms Park before the Wales/England International. (Earlier that week I had bought a long, very expensive suede coat with a big fur collar to wear on the programme.)

The crowd recognised me and started to sing 'Hymns and Arias'. When the interview was over, I ran around to the BBC van and telephoned home. My mother answered and I said 'Mam! Did you see Grandstand and hear the singing?'

'Yes' she replied.

'What did you think of it?' I asked excitedly.

'Oh!' she said, 'Your coat looked lovely.'

CHORUS
And we were singing hymns and arias,
'Land of my Fathers', 'Ar hyd y nôs'.*

We paid our weekly shilling for that January trip:
A long weekend in London, aye, without a bit of kip.
There's a seat reserved for beer by the boys from Abercarn:
There's beer, pontoon, crisps and fags and a croakin'
   'Calon Lan'.

Into Paddington we did roll with an empty crate of ale.
Will had lost at cards and now his Western Mail's for sale.
But Will is very happy though his money all has gone:
He swapped five photos of his wife for one of Barry John.

We got to Twickers early and were jostled in the crowd;
Planted leeks and dragons, looked for toilets all around.
So many there we couldn't budge — twisted legs and pale:
I'm ashamed we used a bottle that once held bitter ale.

Wales defeated England in a fast and open game.
We sang 'Cwm Rhondda' and 'Delilah', damn, they
   sounded both the same.
We sympathized with an Englishman whose team was
   doomed to fail.
So we gave him that old bottle, that once held bitter ale!

He started singing hymns and arias,
'Land of my Fathers', 'Ar hyd y nôs'.

So it's down to Soho for the night, to the girls with the
   shiny beads;
To the funny men with lipstick on, with evil minds
   and deeds.
One said to Will from a doorway dark, damn, she didn't
   have much on.
But Will knew what she wanted, aye . . . his photo of
   Barry John!
'Cos she was singing hymns and arias,
'Land of my Fathers', 'Ar hyd y nôs'.

*'Ar hyd y nôs' = 'All through the night' (not 'Harry's got a horse')

A few years ago I was playing rugby for Glynneath Athletic (they were short), when twenty minutes into the first half we were awarded a penalty. Our full-back, a North Walian by the name of Dyfnallt Morgan, took the kick and his well struck attempt hit the upright.

He shook his head and said 'Bloody Hell!'

The Referee, the Revd. Goronwy Roberts (Llwynhendy), admonished him saying 'There is no need to swear.' Dyfnallt apologised and then a few minutes later we were awarded another penalty. Dyfnallt took great care but unfortunately his second attempt veered away at the last second and struck the other upright.

'Bloody Hell!' he exclaimed.

The Revd. Goronwy Roberts went across to him and said 'I've told you once — there is no need to swear. If you feel the sap of anger rising, just pause for a second and say "Help me Lord" and that moment of anger surely will pass.'

By this time we were losing 16-14 with only minutes to go when we were awarded yet another kick at goal. This time from in front of the posts. The crowd hushed as Dyfnallt with great deliberation made his mark, took three measured steps back, allowed for the cross wind and . . . sliced it!

The ball went skidding away towards the corner flag. Dyfnallt shook his head and was about to say . . . . when he remembered and said 'Help me Lord!'

The skies darkened, there was the sound of a mighty rushing wind and a strange light appeared in the sky. The ball shuddered in flight, changed direction and went between the posts and the Revd. Goronwy Roberts said

'Bloody Hell!'

We lost to referee, say rugby officials

By J. B. G. THOMAS

THAT CONTROVERSIAL disallowed try which robbed Wales of victory at Twickenham on Saturday has led to stern criticism of the Irish referee, Jack West, from Welsh team officials.

Clive Rowlands, the team's coach, said he had no doubts that Wales should have won. "Two controversial decisions by the referee robbed us," he said. "John Williams scored a perfectly good try."

Mr. Jack Young, chairman of the Welsh selectors, agreed that the decision cost his side victory.

"I feel we were robbed by the disallowed try and when the referee neglected to allow advantage when Phil Bennett was making his break that could have led to a score."

NOT CONVINCED

The man who took the ball over the line, winger J. J. Williams, said. "No one will ever convince me that I didn't score a perfectly legitimate try. My hand had touched the ball down."

The incident came in the 29th minute of the second half, from a Gareth Edwards penalty, taken near the halfway line. After a Phil Bennett break the ball passed to prop Phil Llewellyn and then to Delme Thomas who was finally tackled, sending the ball loose.

Williams gathered it up and turned inside towards the posts, short-punting over the heads of the defence and just beating English wings Peter Squires and David Duckham to the ball to touch down for a try. But the referee was not convi[...]

After the match [...] dived for the ball [...] kno[...]

I AM AN ENTERTAINER

'I am an Entertainer' was written following the Welsh defeat at Twickenham in 1974. The referee that day, a Mr John West, an Irishman, disallowed a perfectly good try (in my opinion) by J.J. Williams and Wales were defeated. I had often wondered since writing the poem what Mr West had thought of it, so when I was introduced to him at a dinner I asked him. 'You've given me a sort of immortality' he said, 'but I think it's of a rather dubious kind.' He was a lovely man and he had taken the song in the spirit in which it was meant.

Two years later I was having a quiet drink with some friends in the bar of Glynneath Rugby Club on the eve of the Wales Ireland International at Cardiff. Suddenly the door burst open and four Irish referees burst in with clenched fists shouting 'Where is he? Where is he?' The bar fell quiet, even some of my best friends moved away from me and pretended they were at another table. I slowly got up in that hushed room and said quietly 'Here I am.' The four wild Irishmen looked across and said 'Ah, there you are, what are you having to drink?' They had come over for the match and had come down to Glynneath to invite me to speak at some Referees' Society dinner in Ireland. Unfortunately I was unable to go, but I shall never forget that night in the Rugby Club singing a mixture of Irish and Welsh songs in the bar until the early hours and ending up with 'I Am An Entertainer'.

I am an entertainer and I sing for charity;
For Oxfam and for Shelter, for those worse off than me.
Bangla Desh, Barnardo's Homes. And though I don't
   get paid,
It does one good to do some work for things like
   Christian Aid.

But of all the concerts that I've done for the homeless
   overseas,
The one I did that pleased me most was not for refugees.
'Twas for a home in Ireland that stands amongst the trees:
The sunshine home in Dublin for blind Irish referees!

29

THE DIVINE INTERVENTION

This poem was written some time after it was announced that Phil Bennett had been omitted from the Welsh Squad for the game against England at Twickenham in 1976. The decision to omit Bennett caused a great deal of controversy in Wales. People in his home town of Llanelli were throwing themselves in the canals. I wasn't particularly concerned until I realised some of them had 'tickets' on them. So there I was helping the Red Cross to drag them out — pinching their tickets — and throwing them back in.

Then came the 'Divine Intervention' when both the outside-halves named before Phil were injured and to the great embarrassment of the Welsh selectors Phil Bennett was asked to play against England after all.

I heard it first on 'telly' I thought that sounded odd
Bevan and Dai Richards in and Phil not in the squad
So I 'phoned the Rediffusion man when his number I
    had found
I said 'The picture's all right, but there's something wrong
    with the sound.'

This chap came round in overalls and told me not to fret
He'd change the speaker and the valve and overhaul the set
He'd finished it by Sunday and left me with a laugh
I switched it on, and the fault had gone
It said 'Bennett, outside half.'

Whilst down there in Llanelli the old folk knowing nod
And say recalling Bennett was true an act of God
And a preacher down in Felinfoel spoke in thanks
    and praise
'The Lord,' he said, 'doth often work in strange and
    wondrous ways.'

And he was there at 'Twickers' round collared in the throng
And he knew full well that Wales would win and he raised
    his voice in song
But I spared a thought for England and for their hopes
    and pride
It wasn't really fair to them with God on our side.

But this 'frightfully pucker' English chap thought
    otherwise —
And he knelt in prayer as well
And asked 'Oh Lord let us see a try, we're losing I can tell,
Oh Lord let us see a try, something absolutely twiffic.'
And then 'J.P.R.' scored again and God said 'You should
    have been specific.'

BARRIE THOMAS SPEAKS OUT ON THE BENNETT CONTROVERSY AND SAYS:

Replace Big Five with a supremo

Selectors out! Sack John Dawes! These are the comments which have been echoed around Llanelli since the selectors decided on Sunday to leave Phil Bennett out of the Welsh squad for the England game.

HANDEL GREVILLE said: "The selectors should tell the truth and say he has been disciplined because there can't be any other reason.

"Surely nobody in his right senses would say, as the selectors did, that John Bevan and David Richards are better fly-halves than Bennett at the moment."

These may have been over-emotional comments for supporters annoyed at one of the most ludicrous decisions made in Welsh rugby for years. But I feel the era of the Welsh selectors is coming to an end. Rugby followers are getting sick and tired of unmerited selections for the national team. We in Llanelli are used to it by now.

The time has come to scrap the selectors and replace them with a supremo.

And after listening to John Dawes' explanations for dropping Bennett I would not like to see him as supremo of the Welsh team. The man I think would be an ideal selection to take full charge of the Welsh

team is Carwyn James. If he was made a paid manager of the Welsh team and got rid of his other commitments then I am confident he would make Wales world beaters as he did with the British Lions in New Zealand.

His Scarlets coaching colleague Norman Gale would also be quite capable of doing the job.

Gale has a tremendous rugby know-how as he proved when he coached Scarlets to the cup and championship double a couple of seasons ago.

Bennett's inexplicable ommission from the squad has astounded all leading rugby critics.

In case you have been sleeping the selectors chose Aberavon's John Bevan for the fly-half spot against England with Swansea and Cardiff College of Education's David Richards as substitute.

It is bad enough leaving Bennett out of the team but to leave him out of the squad is the height of stupidity. How can they justifiably leave out a player w[...] as the b[...] world a[...] who is [...] of the [...] sick jo[...]

What[...] selecto[...] ommis[...] said af[...] squad [...] into t[...] and g[...] one [...] chan[...] dese[...]

"I[...] Rich[...] Ben[...]

D[...] mo[...] wh[...] the[...] Ne[...] in[...] W[...] trial. Re[...] Everybody knows the [...] a farce and pointless [...] And to say that Richards is[...]

as good a player as Bennett is absolute rubbish. This was an irresponsible comment from the national coach and does not say much for his judgement.

Bennett's form this season has been brilliant. He has turned defences inside out with his jinking while his line kicking has also been at its very best.

At the moment he is probably playing his best rugby ever. Rugby which was the feature of the British Lions

NORMAN GALE said: "It is unfair to criticise Phil for not playing in the trial. He was desperately keen to play. The long and short of it is why can't Phil have a genuine injury?

"Surely a player is [...]play if

when playing for Scarlets. Many people say he should not play so soon before big matches. But this shows his loyalty to his club. As captain he feels he should play as many games as he can.

I am sure the Barbarians will show how wrong Wales are when they choose the team to play Australia on Monday.

Richards has plenty of promise but at the moment I feel he is very over-rated.

He has plenty of flair and has a bright future ahead of him but at the moment there are a number of better outside-halves than him In Wales apart from Bevan and Bennett.

He is so inexperienced that if he was to play for Wales now it could have nasty consequences on him.

The rest of the Welsh team was selected as expected. Still it is a great shame th[...] another great player. Der[...] Quinnell can not get into [...] Welsh team.

If the selectors keep [...] their baffling and un[...] choices for the Welsh te[...] before long they coul[...] the same position [...] have been during th[...] years. And now is [...] [...] that.

COMMENTS

CARWYN JAMES said: "Phil Bennett is the best fly-half in the world. He has flair and style and that little bit extra God-given skill. To discard Bennett is altogether unbelievable."

PHIL BENNETT said: "What has hurt most is the fact that I was considered the number one fly-half for the Wales game against Australia but now find myself a non-entity."

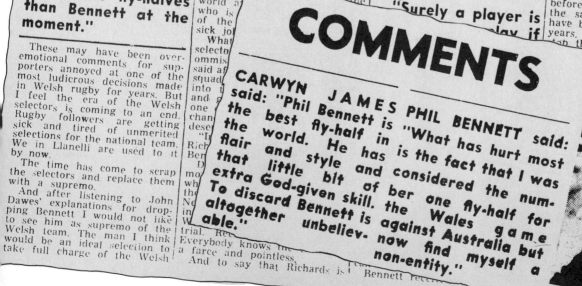

PHIL BENNETT

THE DAY GARETH WAS DROPPED

It was the day of the England/Wales Rugby International in 1978 at Twickenham. A Welsh supporter who was without a ticket was standing outside the ground in the pouring rain. He called up to some English supporters inside the ground, 'What's happening? What's happening?' and was ungraciously told that all the Welsh team with the exception of Gareth Edwards had been carried off injured.

Some five minutes later there came a great roar from the crowd and the Welsh supporter called out again, 'What happened, what happened, Gareth scored has he?'

This next poem inspired by the same blinding faith was written at the time when Gareth seemingly like good wine was improving with age.

A man came home off afternoons and found his child in woe
And asked him 'What's the matter bach, pray tell what
    ails you so
Your little eyes are swollen red, your hands are white
    and shaking'
'Oh! Dad' he said 'I've got bad news, my little heart
    is breaking
Gareth Edwards has been dropped, 'twas on the news
    just now
The Welsh selectors must be mad, there's bound
    to be a row'
His father said 'Now dry your eyes and don't get in a state
Let's be fair mun after all — the man is seventy eight!'

33

THE FRENCH TRIP

Now we booked to fly to Paris on a private plane
    from Rhoose
We noticed over Llantwit that the engine bolts were loose
So when we landed safely, the boys were all so glad
We had a whip round for the driver, first one he'd ever had.

So he took us to this café, a place called Mont Marence
I asked 'Could I see the menu please, I'll order for
    my friends'
I ordered 'Escargots' and chips, from a waiter dressed
    in tails
But Will complained and sent his back and said 'They taste
    like snails'.

Then we drove to 'Parc la Princes' where Wales
    defeated France
I read it in the paper that we didn't have a chance
So when the game was over, all the boys were keen to see
The Follies, Moulin Rouge, Pigalle and the lights of
    gay Paree

We then went down this night club, it wasn't very far
In a sleazy street called 'Rue de Mour' to a place
  called Shangrila
(*There was a red light outside and Dai said*
'Look — there's a Fair')

This woman in the doorway her dress slit to the knee
She said to me 'Hello big boy' — she'd seen me in the sea
(*Then she led me up this creaking stairway to a dimly lit room*
and I thought lucky Mam put in a clean pants and vest . . .)

There she put some records on and music filled the air
She kissed me on the forehead ran her fingers through
  my hair
Her voice was low and husky, she said 'What would you
  like my brave?'
I said 'Have you got Treorchy, singing Diadem or Llêf'

And then the door it opened and a girl came in with Ben
I would see the way he looked at me he'd never go again
(*His little legs were sticking out of his underpants like two*
sticks of celery sticking out of a carrier bag.)

She turned to Ben all slowly and said 'Come sit by me'
And moved a velvet cushion from a leopard skin settee
She called the girl with me across, the one who owned
  the flat,
And said, pointing at Ben, 'If you don't eat your cabbage,
  you'll get to look like that.'

We flew home in the morning Ben's wife was waiting there
She was waiting on the tarmac with curlers in her hair
She asked him things like 'where you been' and about the
  things he'd done
And she found him out without a doubt — 'cos he told her
  France had won.

Graham Price, the Pontypool and Wales prop forward was led off the field with a 'gouged eye' after playing against the French at Cardiff. This Pontypool supporter, Mel Thomas, incensed at what had happened waited for the guilty French forward outside his hotel, intending to settle the score.
However when he came face to face with this huge French forward he was a bit taken aback.
'Hey, mon ami' he said, 'you didn't do that to Pricey on purpose did you?'
'Oui', replied this brute of a man towering above him.
'Right!' said Mel. 'Right! You wait until the spring when you come to Pontypool on your bike, you won't sell a bloody onion!'

One other time when we were in France one of my pals Idris was condemned to death by the guillotine (another case of mistaken identity).
There we were on the Monday morning after the match in this French prison 'Bastille Louis XV'. This French guard with a black hood over his head approached Idris and said (in French) 'It is the tradition of this prison to grant the condemned prisoner one last request before he dies — what is your request?'
Idris thought for a moment and then he said 'I am a proud Welshman and I'd like to sing a song before I die.'
The French guard nodded, 'You are a brave man, monsieur. You may sing your song.'
And there in that Bastille surrounded by cold, grey, unfriendly walls, Idris began to sing:
'One hundred thousand million green bottles . . .'

When I visited Madame Tussauds in London a few years ago, I was amazed to see these large life-size wax-models of the Welsh Rugby team being loaded into a freightliner container marked 'URGENT — for the attention of the English Selectors, Twickenham'.
I enquired what they intended doing with them and was told the English selectors had ordered them and were going to install them at Twickenham. The English team were then going to practise tackling and sidestepping them. Intrigued, I rang the chairman of the English selectors and asked him how the new training method was going.
'Not very well,' he said, 'Wales won 14-6!'

During a Rugby International at Cardiff with singing ringing from the terraces an American tourist turned to some Welsh supporters and asked in a real Southern drawl 'Where is this choir from?'

One of the lads laughed 'They're not a choir. They're just ordinary supporters like us.'

'Tell me then,' asked the Yank, 'where are you from?'

'Oh!' he said, 'I'm from Llangyfelach.'

'Yeah' the Yank went on, 'but what State, what zip code?'

The Welsh supporter turned to me and asked (in Welsh) 'What is this one talking about — I've told him once, I'm from Llangyfelach!'

'Oh!' I explained. 'What you perhaps don't realise is that this chap's from America and he's probably never heard of Llangyfelach?'

'Damn! I didn't think of that,' he said, so he went back to the Yank and told him 'I'm from Llangyfelach . . . three miles from Morriston.'

When I was in Australia during the Welsh Rugby Tour of 1978 I met a remarkable Welshwoman who came to every concert I appeared in and to every game that Wales played in Australia. On the eve of the last test in Sydney she turned up at the theatre with two warm Welsh faggots for me. When I thanked her, she explained that she also had thirty more for the Welsh team and asked where the team were staying. I told her and she went round there at half past eight on the Saturday morning before the game with thirty warm Welsh faggots. Clive Rowlands, the team manager, accepted the gift and assured her that the 'boys' would have them for breakfast.

As events turned out we lost the last test and in the after match function the first person I met was this woman, her eyes all swollen red, tears streaming down her face.

'Oh! Max!' she said. 'Did you see the game?'

I answered that I had and told her not to be upset.

'Oh! Max!' she said, 'Do you think it was the faggots?'

9-3

Anyone who was at Stradey Park, Llanelli on that damp October day in 1972, when Llanelli defeated New Zealand's mighty All Blacks by nine points to three will surely never forget the incredible atmosphere at the ground or indeed the scenes that followed that historic win by the 'Scarlets'.

And when I'm old and my hair turns grey
And they put me in a chair
I'll tell my great grandchildren
That their Datcu* was there.

It was on a dark and dismal day
In a week that had seen rain,
When all roads led to Stradey Park
With the All Blacks here again.
They poured down from the valleys,
They came from far and wide;
There were twenty-thousand in the ground
And me and Dai outside!

The shops were closed like Sunday,
And the streets were silent still.
And those who chose to stay away
Were either dead or ill.
But those who went to Stradey, boys,
Will remember till they die
How New Zealand were defeated,
And how the pubs ran dry.

Oh, the beer flowed at Stradey
(Piped down from Felinfoel),
And the hands that held the glasses high
Were strong from steel and coal.
And the air was filled with singing,
And I saw a grown man cry.
Not because we'd won
But because the pubs ran dry!

Then dawned the morning after
On empty factories.
But we were still at Stradey —
Bloodshot absentees.
But we all had doctors' papers
And they all said just the same:
That we all had 'Scarlet Fever',
And we caught it at the game!

Now all the little babies
In Llanelli from now on
Will be christened Ray or Carwyn,
Derek, Delme, Phil or John.
And in a hundred years again
They'll sing this song for me.
Of when the scoreboard read 'Llanelli 9,
Seland Newydd 3'.

And when I'm old and my hair turns grey,
And they put me in a chair,
I'll tell my great-grandchildren
That their Datcu was there.
And they'll ask to hear the story
Of that damp October day,
When I went down to Stradey
And I saw the 'Scarlets' play.

*Grandfather

ASSO ASSO YOGOSHI

'Asso Asso Yogoshi' was written to coincide with the Japanese Rugby team's visit to Wales. They were extremely popular on and off the field. Before they returned home I asked one of them what he considered was the highlight of the tour. He replied in broken English 'Highlight of tour was Cardiff Arms Park when Welsh clowd were slinging special song for Japanese tourlist telling stoly of little valley in Japan where they make all the Japanese motor bikes.'
I asked 'What song was that?' He replied 'Cwm Honda.'

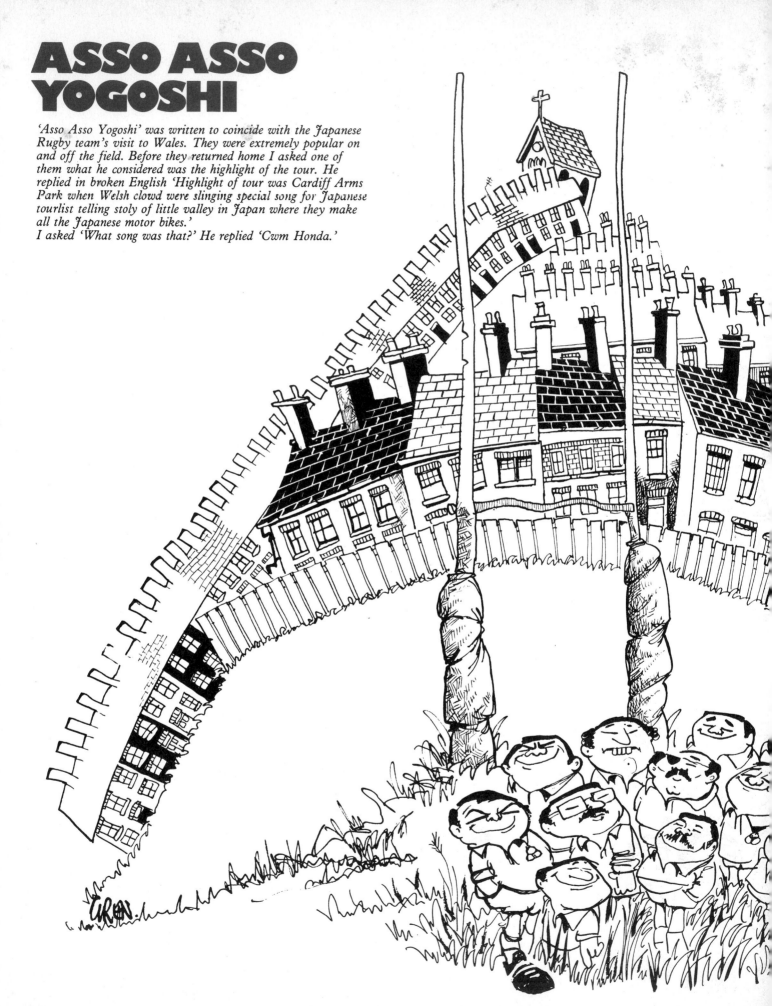

We play Wales on Lugby tour,
It long way from Tokyo.
Learn 'Cwm Rhondda' if we can:
Teach to little children in Japan.

CHORUS
Asso asso yogoshi;
Me Welsh-speaking Japanese.

In Penyglaig we play first game:
Papers say we not to blame.
Gareth Edwards got velly long pass
But not as long as Penygraig grass!

Western Mail say we too small:
We can't get no ball at all.
But we eat bamboo shoots to grow:
Fit platform boots to second row!

But we build big new factorlies,
Filled with plastic surgeries.
Next time we come you no laugh:
We have nine-foot outside half!

Next time we come from Japan
We'll have velly, velly seclet plan.
Seclet plan, man, we can't wait:
Kung Fu he train to be number eight!

Tommy David, he velly big man:
None like him out in Japan.
But when we found we couldn't stop
We give him ** Karate chop.

When we lost we did not flown:
Geisha girls will lub us down.
Gareth Edwards asked me, please,
Next time can he play for Japanese!

So my buy plesent if I can
For wife back home out in Japan.
She opened box, find something long:
Little Welsh doll made in Hong Kong!

41

When David Morris played for the combined Neath and Aberavon side that lost 43-4 to New Zealand in 1973 I wrote:

They didn't leave the score up long
We chipped in for a wreath
Neath blamed Aberavon
And Aberavon, Neath
Some there blamed the linesman
Some blamed you and I
We all blamed the committee
But no one there blamed Dai.

I have always thought it was a great shame that he was never selected for the British Lions. Although he was forced to retire from the International scene with a knee injury it is typical of David Morris that he is as enthusiastic as ever; he is still enjoying his rugby with the newly formed village side Rhigos. Perhaps there have been more famous players, but none that are more respected than this gentle man of rugby who's known to all as 'Dai': a shy, unassuming person who gave his everything at all times, asking for nothing in return. He is one of the most 'genuine' people I have ever met, which is why I admire him more than any other player I know.

DAI MORRIS

Now Dai works down at Tower
In a pit called number four,
Some say that he was quarried
From rock a mile below,
He goes to work each morning
Much the same as you or I,
The foreman calls him Mister
But the children call him Dai

Some say that Dai was much too small
This man who works with iron
And that's the reason why they say
He was never made a Lion
And though they never picked him
'Na fe bois, Felna mae'*
There's none that's played
Though light he weighed
More 'genuine' than Dai.

* That's how it goes.

THE PONTYPOOL FRONT ROW

This song was written as a tribute to the 'Pontypool Front Row' — Charlie Faulkner, Bobby Windzor and Graham Price — who, as well as playing for their club, Pontypool, went on to play with great success for Wales and the British Lions.

Now I'll tell you all a story
About some lads I know.
Who're known throughout the valleys
As the Pontypool Front Row.
It's got a little chorus
And that chorus you all know.
So tell me are you ready?
Up-and-under here we go!

CHORUS
Up-and-under, here we go.
Are you ready, yes or no?
Up-and-under here we go:
It's the song of the Pontypool Front Row.

Now they made a film in London,
It was censored double-X.
The sort of film that frightens one,
Not one of lust and sex.
Mary Whitehouse saw it
And now they'll never show
A film called *Up-and-Under*
Starring the Pontypool Front Row!

We had trouble in Uganda
With President Amin.
So they sent an envoy out there
With a message from the Queen.
To stay that execution
But Amin answered 'No!'
Till a card was sent from the Viet Gwent —
The Pontypool Front Row!

They've had trouble on the railways
With some of soccer's fans.
I've seen them on the terraces
Throwing stones and cans.
They've stopped the soccer specials;
It's a waste of time I know,
'Cos in the end they'll have to send
For the Pontypool Front Row!

There's a programme on the telly,
I watch it when I can,
The story of an astronaut,
The first bionic man.
He cost six-million dollars,
That's a lot of bread I know,
But Wigan offered more than that
For the Pontypool Front Row!

IF

IF you can keep your head when all about you
Are losing theirs and blaming it on you
If you can trust yourself when all the crowd doubt you
And wonder why you blew
If you can wait and not be tired of waiting
For tempers to subside
Or being hated – don't give way to hating
Or favour either side

If you can play advantage and bear the crowds derision
And the offer of new glasses as they question each decision
If you can make one heap of all your expenses
And risk it on the bandit
And lose by holding 'cherries' and admit you – didn't understand it

If you can force your heart and nerve and sinew
To serve your turn when you know your legs have – gone
And keep up with play and hope and pray
Some second row will knock on

If you can talk with crowds and keep your virtue
Or walk with our committee
And not lose the common touch
Neither foes or toilet rolls can hurt you
All our boys are with you – but none *too* much

If you can control that unforgiving minute
With tempers running high
With a calmness born of knowing why – you disallowed that try
If you can watch the moment all again
When they show the game that night
And watch the replay all slowed down
And admit the crowd were right

THEN if you 'Ref' that side again
And you're remembered as '*the one*'
I'd get escorted from the ground
If I were you – my son

46

THE DECK OF CARDS

During the latter part of last season, a bunch of students had been on a long sponsored walk. They arrived in a little town called Ystrad.

The next day being Tuesday, some of the boys went training. A Welsh Rugby Union coach commanded the boys in training, and after he had outlined various scrummaging techniques, he told them to take out their Welsh Rugby Union handbook.

Those of the boys who had Welsh Rugby Union handbooks, took them out. But one boy had only a deck of cards, and so he spread them out.

The coach saw the cards and said 'Boy, put away those cards!' After the training session was over the boy was taken away, and taken in front of the Welsh Rugby Union.

Bill Clement said: 'Why have you brought this boy here?'

'For playing cards in a training session, sir.'

'And what have you to say for yourself, son?'

'Much, sir!'

And Bill Clement said 'I hope so. For if you haven't I will punish you more severely than any boy was ever punished.'

The boy said 'Sir, I have been away in college for six months and had with me neither Welsh Rugby Union handbook or my Ray Williams coaching leaflets!

'But I hope to satisfy you, sir, with the purity of my intentions.'

And with that the boy began his story:

'You see sir, when I look at the ace, it reminds me there is but one game: Rugby Football! And the ace also reminds me of Eddie Waring when he goes "Eh, eh, it's an up-and-under."

When I see the two, it reminds me that there are two codes of Rugby, Rugby Union and Rugby ******

When I see the three, I think of the Viet Gwent: the Pontypool Front Row. Charlie Faulkner, Bobby Windsor and Graham Price.

When I see the four, it reminds me of the four Home Countries: Wales, Scotland, Ireland and England.

When I see the five, I think of the big five: three were wise and picked Dai — and two were foolish and picked Cobner! (They weren't really but it fits!)

When I see the six of course I think of Dai Morris.

When I see the seven, I think of the Snelling Sevens at the end of each season.

When I see the eight I think of the great Mervyn Davies, the greatest 'number eight' in the world.

And of course when I see the nine I think of — Gareth Edwards? No, Dai Morris upside-down!

When I see the ten it reminds me of the years I worked in the Outside-Half Factory, producing that self-same number ten.

When I see the jack, or the knave, or the devil I think of the Rugby League scouts.

When I see the queen I think of Her Majesty Queen Elizabeth, who bestowed on the great Gareth Edwards the MBE. (Some people will do anything for tickets!)

When I see the king, it reminds me of the player they once called 'the King' — Barry John.

When I count the number of spots on my deck of cards I find 365: the number of points we've scored against England in the last couple of games at Cardiff!

There are 52 cards in a pack: the number of people who come and see Pontardulais on Saturdays!

There are four suits: the number of weeks in a month.

There are twelve picture cards: the number of times Wales have won the Triple Crown.

There are thirteen tricks: the number of times they'll have won it by this time next year! (And I was right.)

So you see, sir, my pack of cards serves me not only as an almanac but as a Welsh Rugby Union handbook.'

And friends, that story is true. I know, 'cos I was that boy!

THE OUTSIDE-HALF FACTORY

I'll tell you all a story, 'tis a strange and a weird tale:
Of a factory in my valley, not fed by road or rail.
It's built beneath the mountain, beneath the coal and clay.
It's where we make the outside-halves, that'll play for Wales one day.

Down by the council houses, where on a quiet day
You can hear the giant engines digging up the clay.
No naked lights or matches where the raw material's found
In the four-foot seams of outside-halves, two miles below the ground.

We've camouflaged the mouth with stones, from Northern Bradford spies:
From plastic 'E-Type' Englishmen with promise in their eyes.
And we've boarded up the entrance for the way must not be shown;
And we'll tell them all to **** off and make their ******* own!

My Dad works down in arms and legs where production's running high.
It's he that checks the wooden moulds and stacks them forty high,
But he's had some rejects lately, 'cos there's such a big demand;
So he sells them to the northern clubs, and stamps them 'second-hand'.

It's there where Harry Dampers works, it's where the money's best,
But now his health is failing and the dust lies on his chest.
But he'll get his compensation though his health's gone off the rails
When he sees that finished product score the winning try for Wales.

But now the belts are empty, came a sadness with the dawn.
And the body-press is idle, and the valley's blinds are drawn.
Disaster struck this morning when a fitter's mate named Ron
Cracked the mould of solid gold, that once made Barry John.

Old Harry Dampers (struck with grief), received the final call.
And old Harry has been taken to the greatest outside-half of all.
Whose hands are kind and gentle, though they bear the mark of nails,
So Harry stamped him 'Number Ten', 'cos he was made in Wales.

And the wheels will go on turning, and trams will run on rails,
To that factory 'neath the mountain making outside-halves for Wales.

THE BALLAD OF MORGAN THE MOON

The Americans claim they were the first to land on the moon. This song argues differently and tells the story of that pioneering pipe fitter, Morgan Jones, who was known throughout the valley as 'Morgan the Moon'.

Old Mog the mechanic, I remember him well.
He once built a rocket, or so they will tell,
From an old winding-engine he found on the dole,
Built in the Rhondda and powered by coal.

And when it was finished he painted it red,
And he called it 'Bethania', or so it is said.
And he took it up a mountain on a night late in June
'To get that bit closer,' said Morgan the Moon.

Sleepy Treorchy was bathed in white light
When the shuddering hulk took off in the night.
A deafening scream and then a great roar,
And up past the houses old Morgan did go.

His heat-shield was glowing like anthracite coal
And we prayed down in Cardiff, in mission control.
The barrow-wheels dropped as was previously planned
And old Morgan prepared for Bethania to land.

He landed like linen on a crusty old crater:
Dai said he'd get there lunar or later!
So off Morgan went in the moon's swirling dust,
To collect some rock samples from a crater's hard crust.

A strange piece of rock soon old Morgan found,
Just lying there shining on the dust-covered ground.
He picked it up closely and he let out a call
'Cos written right through it in Welsh was 'Porthcawl'!

I have always enjoyed writing and performing humorous, topical songs; so when the 'New Wave' swept through Britain, 'Johnny Mildew and the Scum' were formed. (The first Welsh Punk Band.)

It was a complete departure from anything I had previously written and we all had great fun recording the song for my 'In Concert' television series. However some people took it seriously and after the programme was transmitted I received letters begging me 'not to change'. I found it unbelievable that it could be taken seriously, but then even my aunt remarked after watching the programme: 'I didn't like that group you had on with you last week.'

Now I was born in Merthyr.
I didn't want to stay
There was nowhere I could go
There was nowhere I could play
So we moved away to Cardiff
To where they'd understand
That we were a 'New Wave Punk Rock Band'

We got ourselves an Agent
A Dowlais man named Dai
He got us an audition
With a chap from E.M.I.
He said 'We'll give you kids a break
The public's kinda dumb
And we'll call you Johnny Mildew
And we'll call the band "The Scum".'

We played the pubs in Cardiff
To earn ourselves some bread
I wore my trousers inside out
And dyed my hair all red
I wrote myself some songs
Like *I'm into Sniffing Glue*
And *I love you so much Baby —*
I could spit all over you!

I wore my Punk Rock clothes
Chains and safety pins
And made a coat from stuff
That they use to line the bins
I stood in a shop doorway
With a pin right through my lip
And a refuse lorry saw me
And I ended on a tip.

We brought a record out last week
I couldn't understand
The BBC won't play it
Producers had it banned
The chorus is offensive
Some words they'll have to 'bleep'
It goes '* * * * * * * * * * *'

Our record contract's folded
They've had enough I guess
But we've had offers from the States
To sign for C.B.S.
We'll make a big impression
When we get over there
We'll scream abuse
And spill our juice
And tell them — 'We don't care'.

* Publisher's note: This line has been censored.

JOHNNY MILDEW AND THE SCUM

One evening in Pontardulais I saw an old man pointing up to the sky and I overheard him ask his friend 'Is that the sun or the moon?' 'I'm not sure,' his friend replied, 'we'd better ask that man over there in the bus shelter.'
They approached the man and one of them asked 'Excuse me, but can you tell us, is that the sun or the moon?'
'I'm not sure,' replied the man, 'I'm from Port Talbot!'

AS DEW FRESH KISSED THE MORNING

I rose at dawn's first waking light
And wandered midst the flowers
And longed that you were by my side
In that morning's early hours
To take your hand and walk awhile
And see the new day dawning
And to kiss you gently on your cheek
As dew fresh kissed the morning.

DID YOU UNDERSTAND?

'Did You Understand?' was a song written during the Miners' Strike of 1972, the first of two strikes which were directly responsible for the defeat of the Conservative Party in the general election that followed.
I remember singing at the time in a village hall in Llanelli. It was a time when the supply of electricity was being rationed to conserve the coal stocks at the power stations. Half-way through the concert the supply to the hall was cut off, leaving us without any means of amplification or lighting.
I remember singing this song in that hall in complete darkness that night with just an acoustic guitar. I knew from the reaction to the song that the public sympathy in the town of Llanelli lay entirely with the collier at that time.

I remember the time of the collier and the candle,
Of a long bitter fight that darkened the land.
And I asked you the question but you wouldn't answer,
When I asked you the question did you understand?
Collier laddie, collier boy.

I saw mills and machines, all lying there idle,
A million or more unemployed in the land.
And I asked them the question but they wouldn't answer
When I asked them the question did they understand?
Collier laddie, collier boy.

Then I saw the ones sit in the seats of decision;
They sat and they judged the miners' demand.
And they all heard the case of the lowly-paid miner,
But though they decided, did they understand?
Collier laddie, collier boy.

Then I saw an old collier, whose body lies broken,
Claimed by the dust much finer than sand.
And I asked him the question, though now he can't answer,
I'll ask him the question and he'll understand.
Collier laddie, collier boy.

BUGEILIOR GWENITH GWYN

WATCHING THE WHITE WHEAT

William Hopkin (known as 'Will Hopkin' the bard) was born at Llangynwyd in 1700. The tradition of Ann Thomas's hapless love for him (The Maid of Cefn Ydfa) is widely 'known in Wales, especially in Glamorganshire. The bard wrote many songs in her honour, but the most popular is 'Bugeilio'r Gwenith Gwyn' 'Watching the White Wheat' sung to the melody previously known as 'Yrhen Gelynen'. It comes from the folk song collection of Miss Jane Williams, Aberpergwm, Glynneath.

Mi sydd fachgen ieuanc ffôl.
Yn byw yn ol fy ffansi.
Myfi'n bugeilio'r gwenith gwyn,
Ac arall yn ei fedi.
Pam na ddendi ar fy ol,
Ryw ddyddar ôl ei gilydd?
Gwaith r'wy'n dy wel'd, y feinir fach,
Yn lanach, lanach beunydd!

Glanach lanach wyt bob dydd,
Neu fi sy'm ffydd yn ffolach.
Er mwyn y gŵr a wnaeth dy wedd,
Gwna im drugaredd bellach:
Cwnn dy ben gwêl acw draw.
Rho i mi'th law wen dirion;
Gwaith yn dy fynwes berth ei thro.
Mae allwedd clo fy nghalon!

Tra fo dwr y mor yn hallt,
A thra fo ngwallt yn tyfu
A thra fo calon dan fy mron
Mi fydda'n ffyddlon iti:
Dywed i mi'r gwir dan gêl
A rho dan sêl attebion,
P'un ai myfi neu arall Ann
Sydd oreu gan dy galon.

AR LAN Y MOR

BY THE SEA SHORE

'Ar lan y Môr (By the Sea Shore) is a lovely traditional Welsh folk song in which the writer tells of how he used to meet the girl he loved by the sea shore where there were red roses (rhosys cochion) and white lilies (lilis gwynion), and where rosemary and thyme grew amongst the rocks.

Some words I once wrote roughly translate the second verse and, hopefully, convey some of the feeling.

Along the shore we walked together
Where thyme grows wild amongst the heather
'Twas there we whiled away the hours
Where all the rocks are strewn with flowers

In the song he goes on to say that although now the girl he loves is far across the sea, his thoughts are always with her.

Ar lan y môr mae rhosys cochion
Ar lan y môr mae lilis gwynion
Ar lan y môr mae nghariad inne
Yn cysgu'r nos a chodi'r bore

Ar lan y môr mae carreg wastad
Lle bum yn cyfarfod gynt am cariad
Oddeutu hon mae teim yn tyfu
Ac ambell sbrigyn o rosmari

Tros y môr y mae fy nghalon
Tros y môr y mae f'ochneidion
Tros y môr y mae f'anwylyd
Sy'n fy meddwl i pob munud

SIRHOWY HILL

'Sirhowy Hill' is a song which gets its title from the valley of the same name. It was written while I was reflecting on the threatened closure of the steel works in the South Wales valleys near Tredegar and Ebbw Vale. The fact that flowers were growing again on the hills was no compensation to the steelworker faced with unemployment, but was proof in itself that the wheel had turned full circle for the men of a valley long forged in a skill.

A steel town was waking as dawn it was breaking
And talk was uneasy 'bout things at the Mill
And talk is uneasy in the streets of the valley
For flowers are growing on a Sirhowy Hill.

CHORUS
For the wheel is full turning
And flowers are learning
To grow once again
On a Sirhowy Hill.

62

I wandered my way on that shabby old morning
In a broken old valley where the pitwheel is still
Where tired old terraces built in a hurry
Are painted so gaily on a Sirhowy Hill.

The smoke and the sulphur I knew as a lad
On thinking it over, it wasn't that bad
So let those old furnaces do what they will
Now flowers are growing on Sirhowy Hill.

Those hills that were crippled of hawthorn and heather
Of fern and of flower strangely are still
For the wheel is full turning and flowers are learning
To grow once again on Sirhowy Hill.

They'll sit and decide in the seats of decision
On the fate of a valley should the furnaces chill
And offer new work in some marshmallow factory
To men of a valley long forged in a skill.

ABERFAN

A shy and fragile leaf now greens,
In a bright and plastic room
On tender stem it offers forth
To cast its earthen womb
Fed by a valley's tears
That watched it leaf and grow
To tell of ones that sleep the night
In Aberfan below

One day those sleepy flowers
Will leave that sunsealed land
And wink away the night
That no one understands
To tell us why that summer fades
In a single afternoon
And why that day in Aberfan
Did autumn come so soon.

SLOW-MEN AT WORK

*If I was to ask who the hardest working men in Britain today
are no doubt some would say, the collier or the trawlerman in
icy seas, but in my opinion the hardest working men must be
the 'council roadmen'.*

*I remember it was a bitterly cold January morning and I
happened to pass some council roadmen. Some of them (if not
all of them) were leaning on their shovels shivering. I called out
'Why don't you do some work to keep warm?'*

One of them shouted back 'I'd rather be cold than tired.'

*Then there was another occasion when I passed a hole in the
road from which I could hear council roadmen singing 'Happy
birthday to you, happy birthday to you'. I enquired whose
birthday it was, and was told 'It's the hole's; he's one today.'*

*My favourite council roadman story however concerns the
foreman who smashed his shovel down on a poor defenceless
snail. When he was asked why had he done it, he answered
'He's been following me all day.'*

*This song was written in tribute to the men whose shoulders are
always to the wheel: the council roadmen. The idea for the song
was suggested to me by one of their signs which read 'SLOW —
MEN AT WORK'.*

There is a band of loyal men
Who come in their lorries but they don't say when.
What they do, well I just can't say —
They're either coming or they're going away.

CHORUS
And they keep their billy-cans brewing,
They keep their billy-cans brewing.
They keep their billy-cans brewing
And they brew a little more each day!

But it's a dangerous job both cruel and hard;
They risk their lives when the floods are bad.
One drowned last week whilst clutching his spade:
He slipped and he fell in the tea he'd made!

Have you seen them working on the road,
Sweating and toiling with a heavy load?
Seen them working with no thought of tea?
Well if you have you don't live by me!

They say that Rome wasn't built in a day,
And there was one big long delay,
The reason was and it's a fact,
The council had the main contract!

GREEN GREEN FIELDS

This song, a parody on the Tom Jones' hit 'The Green Green Grass of Home', was written in protest at the decision to drive the extension of the 'Heads of the Valley' motorway through the Pontneathvaughan cricket ground. The 'Bont' as it is called was the club I played with for many years and is reputed to be one of the oldest in Wales.
It was a great shame, therefore, to see that road driven unnecessarily through such a lovely, picturesque little ground. The club true to its great tradition still flourishes, but sadly cricket is no longer played in the village of 'Pontneddfechan'.

Now it's never been the same
Since that news from London came,
Games are cancelled now but not for any rain.
Down Bont Road I look with tears a-falling,
'Cos I can see bulldozers crawling,
Why can't they leave our Green Green Field alone?
  But they'll bring that ugly concrete highway,
  To take away what once was my way,
  Why can't they leave our Green Green Field alone?

The old Club House is still standing,
Though the paint is cracked and dry.
And there's that one-armed-bandit that we used to play on.
Down that road I look with tears a-falling,
'Cos I can see a Euclid crawling.
Why can't they leave our Green Green Field alone?

But as I bat and look around me
At the four short legs that surround me,
I realize that surveyor wasn't joking.
'Cos they'll bring that ugly concrete highway
And take away what once was my way.
Why can't they leave our Green Green Field alone?
  Yes, they'll bring that ugly concrete highway
  And take away what once was my way,
  Why can't they leave our Green Green Field alone?

They have thundered through the hills,
Past the streams and watermills.
They have turned our little valley floor to stone.
They have broken through the farms and churches,
Lovely oaks and silver birches.
Why can't they leave our Green Green Field alone?
  But we'll fight although we ain't got money,
  (I've got a Butty in the Free Wales Army!)
  Why can't they leave our Green Green Field alone.

DUW! IT'S HARD

*'Duw! it's hard' (God! it's hard) is a song I wrote after seeing
a supermarket advertised in a local newspaper. The
supermarket's address was given as 'The Old Pit Head Baths,
Ebbw Vale'. The advertisement appeared at the time when
many collieries were being closed in South Wales and it
illustrated the changes that were taking place in the mining
communities at that time.*

*The song has always meant a great deal to me, because my
father was killed in a colliery explosion and I worked for many
years underground myself.*

In our little valley they've closed the colliery down,
And the pithead baths is a supermarket now.
Empty journeys red with rust rolled to rest amidst the dust
And the pithead baths is a supermarket now.

CHORUS
'Cos it's hard, Duw it's hard.
It's harder than they will ever know.
And it's they must take the blame
The price of coal's the same,
But the pithead baths is a supermarket now.

They came down here from London because our output's low,
Brief-cases full of bank clerks that have never been below.
And they'll close the valley's oldest mine, pretending that they're sad.
But don't your worry, Butty bach, we're really very glad.

My clean-clothes-locker's empty now, I've thrown away the key
And I've sold my boots and muffler and my lamp-check one-five-three
But I can't forget the times we had, the laughing midst the fear,
'Cos every time I cough I get a mining souvenir.

I took my old helmet home with me, filled it full of earth
And I planted little flowers there, they grew for all they're worth.
And it's hanging in the glass-house now — a living memory,
Reminding me they could have grown in vases over me.

But I know the local magistrate, she's got a job for me
Though it's only counting buttons in the local factory.
We get coffee breaks and coffee breaks, coffee breaks and tea,
And now I know those dusty mines have seen the last of me.

'Cos it's hard, Duw it's hard.
It's harder than they will ever know.
And if ham was underground would it be twelve bob a pound,
The pithead baths is a supermarket now.
Aye, the pithead baths is a supermarket now.

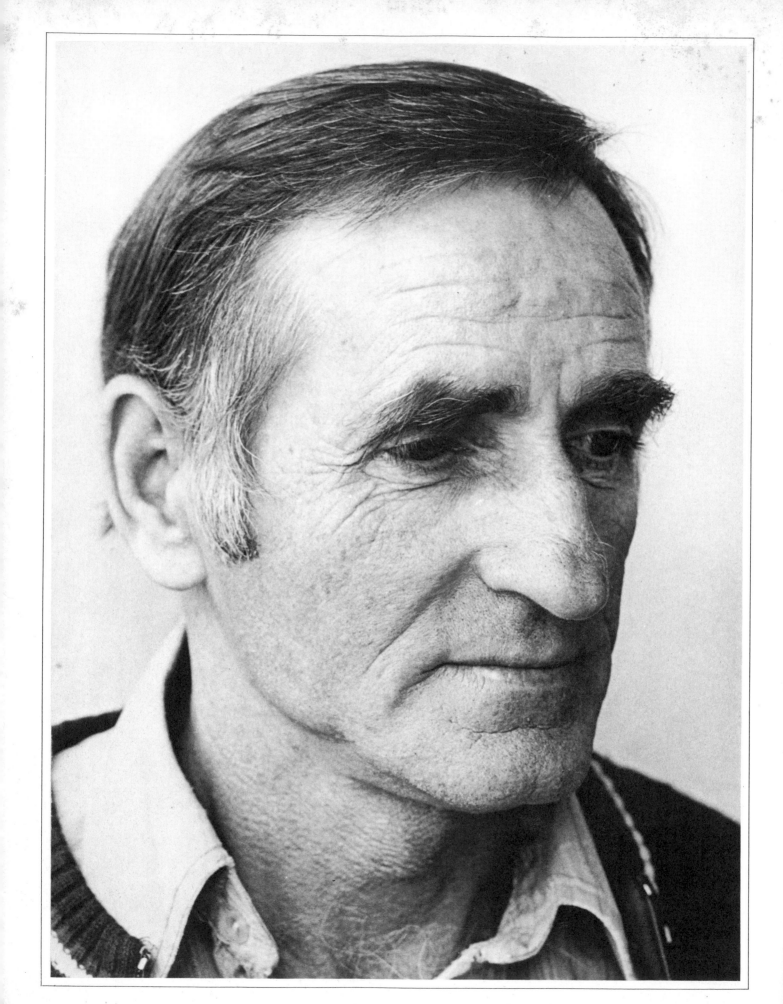

RHONDDA GREY

*'The tools are on the bar' is an old
mining term used commonly in the
South Wales coalfield to signify the end
of the shift, when it was time to 'put
the tools on the bar'. The bar was a
rod of iron on which the collier kept his
tools locked for safety.
This mining expression also became
symbolic of ill-health. Old colliers
taking their grandsons for a walk on
Sunday mornings would be forced to
stop a while to fight for breath because
of 'dust'. 'Wait a minute, bach,' they'd
say, 'the tools are on the bar.'
I have used that expression in a song
which tells about a colour. A colour not
found in the slates or the pavements of
the valley towns but only in the faces
of the old men that once worked in the
mining industry. I've called that colour
and the song — Rhondda Grey.*

One afternoon from a council school
A boy came home to play.
With paints and coloured pencils
And his homework for the day.
'We've got to paint the valley, Mam,
For Mrs Davies' art.
What colour is the valley, Mam?
And will you help me start?'

'Shall I paint the Con. Club yellow,
And paint the Welfare blue?
Paint old Mr Davies red
And all his pigeons too?
Paint the man who kept our ball —
Paint him looking sad?
What colour is the valley, Mam?
What colour is it Dad?'

'Dad, if Mam goes down the shop
To fetch the milk and bread,
Ask her fetch me back some paint —
Some gold and white and red.
Ask her fetch me back some green,
(The bit I've got's gone hard).
Ask her fetch me back some green;
Ask her, will you Dad?'

His father took him by the hand
And they walked down Albion Street.
Down past the old Rock Incline.
To where the council put a seat.
Where old men say at the close of day
' 'Dy'n ni wedi g'neud ein siar'*
And the colour in their faces says
'The tools are on the bar.
The tools are on the bar.'

'And that's the colour that we want
That no shop has even sold.
You can't buy that in Woolies, lad,
With your reds and greens and gold.
It's a colour you can't buy, lad,
No matter what you pay.
But that's the colour that we want:
It's a sort of Rhondda Grey.'

* We've done our share

TEN THOUSAND INSTANT CHRISTIANS

One of the great influences on the Welsh way of life has undoubtedly been the tradition of the 'Chapels'. It is therefore sad to see their decline and sadder still to see them converted into bingo halls and the like.
I remember one Rugby International in which we'd been singing the old Sunday school favourites in the pubs of Cardiff all the morning: 'Rwyn canu fel canar aderyn', 'Draw draw yn China'. Then again at the ground it was Welsh hymns that rang from the terraces: 'Cwm Rhondda' and 'Calon Lan'.
It seemed strangely sad therefore that on the way back from the match we should pass a Chapel with a sign outside which said 'FOR SALE'. Seeing that sign influenced me to write this song.

When He sees the Hope & Anchor where we sang before the game,
Where 'Cwm Rhondda' and 'Delilah' first sounded both the same.
The bar was filled with singing, and the songs came on a tray.
And Saturday was Sunday, I wonder what He'll say?

When He sees the North Enclosure with its belly-full of ale,
And sees that male-voice flagon, sing to the twisted barrier-rail.
'Cwm Rhondda' and 'Penmachno' — hymns of yesterday —
But only half-remembered, I wonder what He'll say.

When He sees those touch-line tenors, with their copies made of sand:
Ten thousand instant Christians, and the Glynneath Silver Band.
'Come on mun, Ref., for Christ sake, the ball was still in play,'
Ten thousand instant Christians, I wonder what He'll say.

When He sees that empty chapel with its locked and shuttered doors,
And sees that dusty Bible, cobweb-covered floors.
The numbers slowly dwindling, much fewer now each day:
Calfaria now a bingo-hall, I wonder what He'll say.

THE TWO SILVER CLOCKS

If ever pride asserts itself it does so in the form of the Welsh male voice choir, especially when in competition. Not in the history of choral singing has any Welsh choir come last — always seventh or eighth, but never last. I remember coming back from Cardigan Eisteddfod with a choir that had come tenth! They had suffered a very critical and cutting adjudication. Upon travelling home in the bus one of the second tenors enquired: 'Who was that adjudicator anyway?'
He was told 'Madame Clare Teifi Jenkins, D.Mus(E), L.R.A.M., F.R.C.M., Ph.D.(Oxon).'
'There you are,' he said 'What does she know about bloody music?'
'The Two Silver Clocks' is the story of the occasion when a certain male voice choir went on a concert tour of Scotland the week before the Rugby International at Murrayfield. The story which you may find hard to believe is to a great extent true.

When a certain male voice choir went on their Scottish Tour
It was decided in committee the Monday night before
There'd be no singing on the bus, no drinking and no noise
Till after Thursday's concert, it was 'Watch your voices boys!'
Now we got there on the Wednesday night our hotel 'The Slanjivar'
We checked into reception and headed for the bar.
The Conductor L.T. Lloyd, J.P., eyes us with a frown
'Not till Friday now, boys, bach don't let the choir down.'
'Wait till he's gone to bed,' I said 'and then we'll have a few.'
But they left the chairman Dick on guard and the Reverend Prydderch Pugh
'Wait till they fall asleep,' I said 'then we'll have a little drink.'
But Dick had been on nights all week and he never slept a wink.
Thursday's concert came at last, 'twas enjoyed by one and all
And this big reception followed in the local village hall.
They presented L.T. with a silver clock to commemorate the Tour
And asked him 'Will you have a dram, a wee one 'fore ye go.'
'Well just the one then,' L.T. said 'It's for the heart you know.'
And then he had another one and then he had some more!
He drank a bottle on his own and slumped down in a chair
And then he said 'I'm feeling bad I'm going to have some air.'
Later, they found him in a toilet, Dick and the Reverend Pugh
He was calling for some Hughie 'Hughie, Hughie, Hugh!'
Then he was sick — all over Dick, then he was sick again
Damn his teeth came out, I tried to shout, but the Reverend pulled the chain.
Dawn broke an hour later with night's last shadows fleeting
L.T. asleep on the toilet seat — and the committee had another meeting.
'He's due at the Civic Hall tonight,' said our secretary Keith
'To speak to the Church Young Women's Guild but he can't without his teeth.'
'Aye,' I said, 'Keith is right, the only thing to do
Is try down at the filter bed, perhaps his teeth came through.'

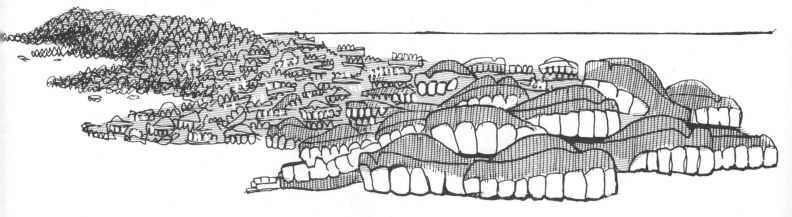

76

Though ill at ease we shuffled down to a man called Matt Muckloo
And the Reverend asked ashamedly 'Have any teeth come through?'
'Oh aye' Matt said 'they're over there behind that box of flowers
But you'll have to try them all I fear, till you find the one that's yours.'
There was this tea chest full of them — in rows all neatly lain
Poor L.T. he tried out three — then he was sick again.
So we took him to a dentist and told him of our plight,
I said 'Can't you give him something? He's got to speak tonight.'
'Well,' he said 'I'll give you these, they were for a Mr Drew
But he's got the same shape head as him, it's the best that I can do.'
We slipped the teeth into his mouth and the Reverend Prydderch Pugh
Said 'That's no use, they're much too loose, we'll have to get some glue.'
So they rushed him to this place in town, it was getting rather late
And we glued them in with 'Evostik', it stuck tiles on my Auntie's grate.
Then we rushed him to this dinner, in the local Civic Hall
The Provost of the town spoke first and welcomed one and all.
And then L.T. was introduced by the Provost's daughter Heather
And no one understood a word — his teeth had stuck together.
We all felt sorry for him — I feel sorry for him still
We told the Church Young Women's Guild that he'd been taken ill,
So they had a collection for him and it came as quite a shock
When L.T. was presented with another Silver Clock.
And they asked him 'Will ye have a dram, a wee one 'fore ye go?'
And the Reverend Pugh said 'No by damn, we've heard that one before.'
Well he got home Sunday with his clocks and his wife said 'How absurd,
Why ever did they give you two?' — and he never said a word.
Now some may not believe my tale — but I don't really care
'Cos it really happened, honest — I know 'cos I was there.

ZULU WAR

There we were at O'Tooles Drift in the Zulu War. Only six men left of an entire regiment; Idris Walters (Bridgend), Ivor Morgan (Briton Ferry), Sergeant Davies, Gareth Owen, me and . . . Ivor Emmanuel.

All around us lay our dead and wounded companions, whilst over the hill encamped in the clearing were two and a half thousand Zulus. Throughout the night the primitive sound of their war drums kept us awake.

At first light Sergeant Davies said 'C'mon boys, one more attack, one last effort.' But it was a lost cause. We were hopelessly outnumbered and no one rallied to the call. 'C'mon' repeated Sergeant Davies. No one stirred. Weary, bloody and bandaged we just lay there, our spirit broken, our flag in tattered shreds.

Then Ivor Emmanuel began to sing:

'Men of Harlech rise to glory
Victory is hovering o'er ye.'

As Ivor's rich baritone voice rang out, courage stirred again
in our hearts and we dragged ourselves up from that
sandbagged, bloodstained hell. The strength returned to our
arms; faith and hope shone again in our eyes. We charged
towards the Zulus, screaming and yelling.

The air filled with assegais, stones and spears and the
blood-curdling screams of the Zulu warriors. The first to fall
was Ivor Morgan, a crudely-carved spear through his chest.
Still Ivor Emmanuel sang 'Men of Harlech' . . .

A large painted stone felled Gareth Owen, then an assegai
impaled Idris Walters — still Ivor Emmanuel sang 'Men of
Harlech'. One by one we fell until the only ones left were
me, Sergeant Davies and . . . Ivor Emmanuel. Then a
wicked curling spear struck Sergeant Davies. As he fell he
turned to Ivor Emmanuel and gasped, 'For God's sake, Ivor
— sing something they know will you!'

MINERS' FORTNIGHT

(ODE TO BARRY ISLAND)

When I was a lad, the last week in July and the first week in August were traditionally 'Miners' Fortnight'. The collieries would close, horses were brought blinking to the surface and whole villages would move some twenty or thirty miles down the road to Porthcawl or Barry Island.
These then are some of my childhood recollections.

I remember 'Miners' Fortnight' when I was just a lad
It was always Porthcawl or Barry Island
And the weather always bad
In a brand new shirt, and shoes that hurt
The ones Mam saved to buy
To go to Barry Island on the last week in July.

We'd catch a bus down by the square —
My bucket in my hand
Then all the fuss to get on the bus
And we always had to stand
Then I'd be sick and my shoes I'd kick
The ones Mam saved to buy
To go to Barry Island on the last week in July.

So they'd put me by the driver for me to have some air
And my mother'd say, 'He's never this way'
And she'd come and comb my hair
Then I'd see the sea and I'd want to pee
If I couldn't I would cry
When I went to Barry Island on the last week in July.

Our caravan 'The Waters Edge' ten miles from the sea
We'd drag the cases over and we didn't have the key
Then, we couldn't light the gas lamp — I've gone and
   marked my tie
When we went to Barry Island, on the last week in July.

I'm on the beach it's Sunday, I've met a friend called Russ
I'll have to buy another bucket — I've left mine on the bus
I've cut my foot — it's bleeding, my cousin says 'You'll die
And they'll bury you in Barry on the last week in July.'

I'm going to the fair tonight, my bucket full of shells
The weather forecast's settled now, with dry and sunny spells
I've bought Mamgu* a present and waved the sea goodbye
My mother's found my plastic mac and the weather's
   nice and dry.

Aye that's how I remember Miners' Fortnight
When I was just a lad
Porthcawl or Barry Island, and the weather always bad.

* Grandmother.

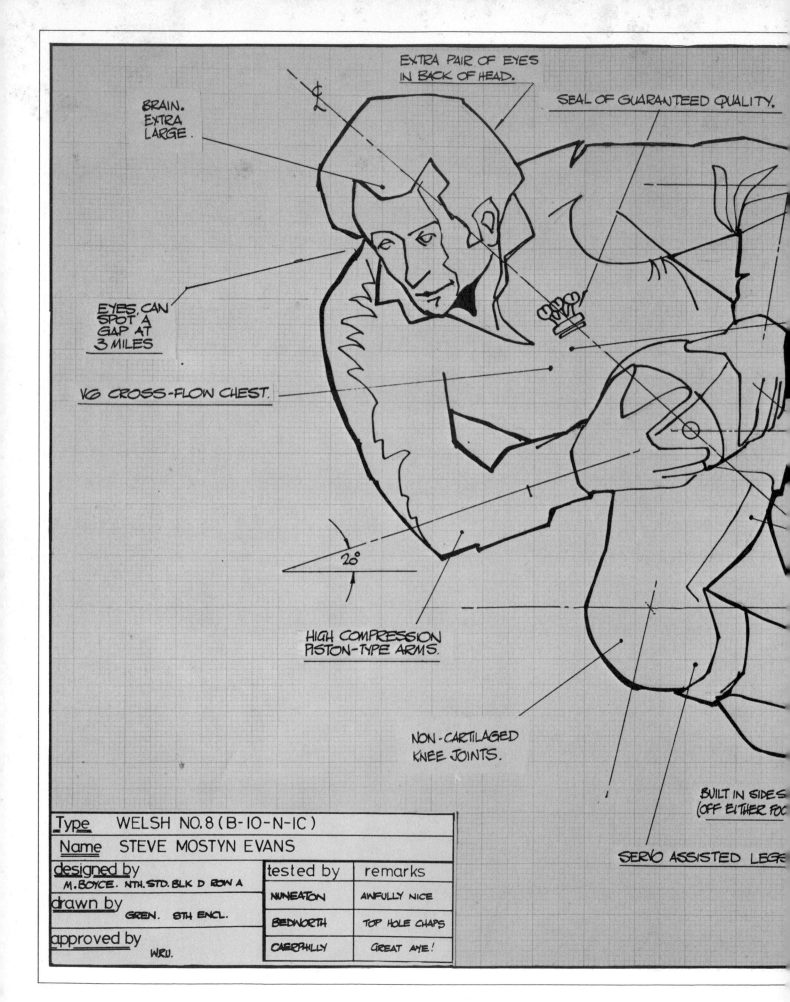

BRAIN. EXTRA LARGE.

EXTRA PAIR OF EYES IN BACK OF HEAD.

SEAL OF GUARANTEED QUALITY.

EYES, CAN SPOT A GAP AT 3 MILES

V6 CROSS-FLOW CHEST.

20°

HIGH COMPRESSION PISTON-TYPE ARMS.

NON-CARTILAGED KNEE JOINTS.

BUILT IN SIDES (OFF EITHER FOO

SERVO ASSISTED LEGS

Type	WELSH NO. 8 (B-IO-N-IC)		
Name	STEVE MOSTYN EVANS		
designed by M. BOYCE. NTH. STD. BLK D ROW A		tested by	remarks
drawn by GREN. 8TH ENCL.		NUNEATON	AWFULLY NICE
		BEDWORTH	TOP HOLE CHAPS
approved by WRU.		CAERPHILLY	GREAT AYE!

82

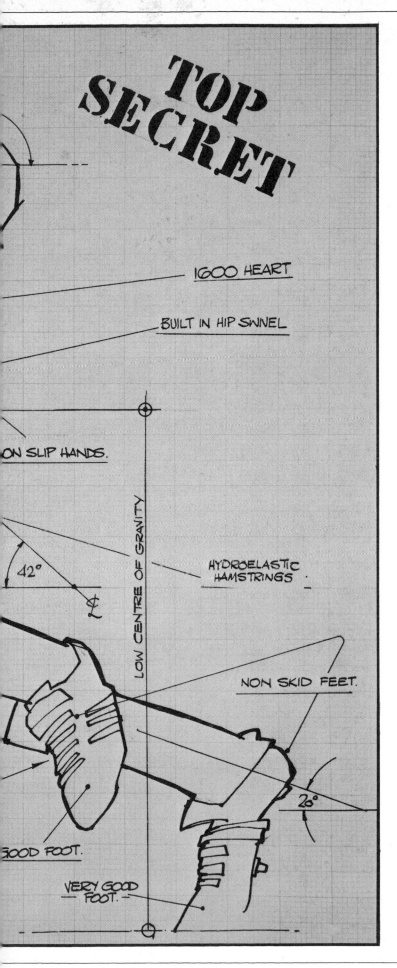

STEVE 'MOSTYN' EVANS

When Steve 'Mostyn' Evans was found unconscious at the bottom of a ruck in a West Wales Rugby Union Cup Match last Saturday, he was rushed to Neath General Hospital. Dr Peregrine Cleggs, the surgeon attending him, issued this statement to his staff:

'Steve "Mostyn" Evans — Rugby player, a man barely alive. Gentlemen, we can rebuild him. We have the technology, we have the capability to make the world's first bionic number eight. Steve "Mostyn" Evans will be that man, better than he was before. Better than even Mervyn Davies was, better, stronger, faster.'

'We have the capability,' said the surgeon Dr Cleggs
'To fit a "1600" heart and servo-assisted legs
An automatic side valve heart that the lab have had on test
And high compression piston arms and a V6 cross-flow chest.'

Steve 'Mostyn' Evans was rebuilt, Cleggs rose to his feet
'We'll try him out on Saturday the tests are all complete
We'll try him first against a side that can easily be beaten.
'Yes!' I said 'a rubbish side, Bedworth or Nuneaton.'

* Or whatever town I'm performing in at the time.

The day was wet and windy and Dr Cleggs he cussed
And threw tarpaulins over Steve, in case his arms would rust
Then they checked his logic patterns and told the student nurse
Not to forget when half time comes — to put him in reverse.

I'll ne'er forget the way he played, the way he handled in the rain
And the way the Committee said 'He won't play here again,
We can't afford to play against him — he'll get the club in debt
He kicked the ball to touch first half — we haven't found it yet.'

Then when the game was over I offered Cleggs a drink
He paused and took a fulsome draught and asked me 'What do you think?'
'Wasn't Steve magnificent, the best, the greatest ever?'
I said 'He's pretty good but a "Mervyn Davies" never.'

83

THE DEVIL'S MARKING ME

I had a dream the other night,
The strangest dream of all,
I dreamt I was in Heaven,
Away from life's hard call.
It was as I'd imagined,
Where peace ruled all serene.
The signs to Heaven were all in Welsh;
Hell's signs were painted green!

   Painted green, painted green.
   The signs to Heaven were all in Welsh;
   Hell's signs were painted green.

I entered through the heavenly gate,
I heard the heavenly band,
And there was John the Baptist
On Barry John's right hand!
He plays for the Heaven Welsh XV,
They're very fit and keen.
We'd play the Heaven English
If they could only raise a team!

   Raise a team, raise a team,
   We'd play the Heaven English
   If they could raise a team.

There was Rugby every morning
On a field of golden corn,
And the referee was Gabriel
And he blew on a silver horn.
They tell me we play Hell next week
In the annual charity,
I wouldn't mind but I've been told
The devil's marking me!

   Marking me, marking me,
   I wouldn't mind but I've been told
   The devil's marking me.

But now my dream has faded
And I wake up to the morn,
I find beneath my pillow
A sheaf of golden corn.
So I know that when I go there,
Beyond death's victory,
I'll take my Rugby jersey
On that Gospel train with me.

   Train with me, train with me,
   I'll take my Rugby jersey
   On that Gospel train with me.

ASHES

Once upon a time in a little village in Surrey there lived a little boy named Jack. He lived with his stepmother, a haughty ugly woman. Now she had two ugly sons who used to bully little Jack and make him get out of bed on cold mornings to clean the grate and light the fire. As he sat there on the hearth amongst the cinders they laughed at him and called him Ashes.

One day the two ugly brothers became very excited. They had received a letter from the Rugby Football Union, telling them they had both been selected for the final English trial.

The stepmother was delighted, she had always hoped that one day one of her sons would play for England.

The day of the trial arrived and the tears ran down Jack's little face as he watched them get into their car and drive to Twickenham.

'I wish I could have a trial,' he said.

Then all of a sudden a strange light appeared in the sky and the room was filled with twinkling stars and moonbeams and a little voice said,

'Don't be afraid Ashes, I am your fairy Godselector and I have come to help you and see that you play in the final English trial too.'

'But I haven't got any boots,' said Ashes, 'and how will I get to the ground?'

The fairy took Ashes into the garden and asked him to get a pumpkin. He brought one to her and she tapped it with her wand. Suddenly it changed into an Austin Allegro with a pair of brand new rugby boots on the back seat.

'Now,' said the fairy 'you can play in the trial too.'

But before he left the fairy warned Ashes that he must return before the clock struck midnight — when all the magic would disappear.

Meanwhile at the final English trial at Twickenham the English selectors were watching without interest the dull, unimaginative play of the probable three-quarters.

Then Ashes ran onto the field and, gathering the loose rolling ball, started to run. The crowd were buzzing with excitement, never before had they seen such a player; he was the sole topic of conversation on the terraces.

After the game was over Ashes was so busy signing autographs in the Clubhouse that he forgot all about his promise to the fairy. All at once he heard a clock striking midnight. He realised what was going to happen at any second. Without any explanation to the English selectors he ran out of the ground across to his car.

The clock continued to strike. He ran as fast as he could. In his haste one of his boots came off. The English selectors ran after him, but just as Ashes reached the gates of the ground the clock struck twelve and the only person left outside the ground was a Traffic Warden sticking a parking ticket on a pumpkin.

The Chairman of the English selectors was heartbroken but he made up his mind to search all over England until he

found the player whose foot fitted the boot. After much searching he finally came to the house where Ashes lived. Whilst the two ugly brothers laughed Ashes tried on the boot. It was a perfect fit. The Chairman of selectors was overjoyed. At last they had found the answer to all their problems.

But then a strange light appeared in the sky. The room was filled with twinkling stars and moonbeams as Ashes' fairy Godselector appeared again.

'I fear sirs,' she said to them,
'Young Ashes cannot play.
His stepbrothers tried to tell you
But you brushed them both away
He cannot play for England'
She waved her wand in anger,
'His father was born in Cardiff
And his mother comes from Bangor.'

Then Ashes said 'I'll play for Wales'
'Twas said with fierce pride
But what with Gareth Edwards
He didn't get in the side.

I was out walking one day and a car stopped and a very 'English' voice called out to this old collier who happened to be passing.

'Hey Dai, come here. How do I get to Carmarthen?'

The old man walked slowly towards the car and asked 'How did you know my name was Dai?'

The frightfully English Englishman replied 'I guessed.'

The old man smiled and said 'Then guess your way to Carmarthen.'

In the colliery in my village every section of the work force was represented by a 'committee man' who served as their spokesman in industrial disputes.

One day the colliers' committee man Ben Thomas went to see the Manager Mr Pocock with a 'case'.

'It's about one of the colliers,' Ben said. 'Mr Harries the Under Manager caught him sitting down in the roadway last Thursday having a drink of water and cropped him half a shift's wages.

'Now this particular man is the hardest working, most conscientious collier in the whole pit. He's first in the face in the morning, clears his own coal, then helps the older men in the gate end to clear theirs, then back with the timber boys to help with the supplies.

'The man never never stops and last week Mr Harries caught him having two minutes rest and cropped him half a shift's wages. I think it's a travesty of justice Mr Pocock.'

Mr Pocock rose slowly to his feet and said 'I agree, Ben — I'm so glad you've brought this case to me attention but don't worry, I'll see this man right, tell him to come and see me.'

And Ben said, 'Here I am Mr Pocock.'

A few days after I had played the Royal Albert Hall in London I appeared in a Rugby club in the village of Brynmawr near Merthyr Tydfil. The organisers were unduly concerned that facilities weren't up to that of the Albert Hall with the result the Ladies' Committee decided to do something about it. One of them, a lovely friendly lady, had some wallpaper left over from decorating her child's bedroom and had decided to paper my dressing room with it. So there I was, surrounded by teddy bears, golliwogs and trains and in the corner, a big heavy iron-clad cooker.

It was in the middle of winter and extremely cold, so they had dragged this cooker from somewhere and turned all the hot plates on full to heat my dressing room. The Chairman came in to enquire if everything was satisfactory. I assured him that it was and thanked him for all his Club's efforts. 'That's all right, Max,' he said, 'If you're still cold — put the grill on.'

You thought because 'twas Christmas
You'd do something so good
You'd help the poor and the needy
Like you always thought you should
So you crept into a neighbour's home
And there against the wall
There stood a lonely Christmas tree
A-leaning 'gainst the wall.
It had no fairy on it
And without it did look bare
And so you climbed up to the top
To make the children stare.
You waited for the morning
Their joyous eyes to see
But you were far too heavy
And you snapped the bloody tree.

CHRISTMAS

It was the tradition in our chapel every Christmas to produce a nativity play, in which all the children took part. One year I played the part of Joseph, Ann Llywellyn was Mary and we borrowed a real donkey from Ty-Nant farm. Our Sunday school teacher built an inn by the pulpit out of cardboard and egg boxes. The innkeeper was Billy Williams (they'd given him a part with very little to say because he was apt to forget his lines).

Christmas Eve arrived and as the children 'behind the clock' sang 'Silent Night' I led the donkey up the centre aisle of the chapel to the inn and said my few lines.

'I am one called Joseph and this is my wife Mary who is with child, have you any room at the inn?'

Billy, who was very nervous and visibly shaking, never said a word. He'd forgotten his one simple line.

The Sunday school teacher waved frantically for me to ask him again. I repeated my line:

'I am one called Joseph and this is my wife Mary who is with child, have you any room at the inn?'

Still no reply from Billy, so I whispered to him 'Make it up, mun!'

That proved the ruination of our nativity play, for when I asked him again was there any room at the inn, he replied 'Yes, plenty of room, c'mon in.'

PWY FYDD YMA 'MHEN CAN MLYNEDD

'Pwy fydd yma 'mhen can mlynedd?' (Who'll be here in a hundred years?) is the recurring refrain of a much loved song chorused in Welsh pubs and chapels. I began by calling it a hymn but actually it's an old Sankey and Moody song translated by a great Welsh hymnologist. You'd understand my mistake if you'd heard it sung as often as I have and accorded it the same reverence as our best loved 'terrace' hymns.

In the part of Wales where I was born and bred Rugby Football stirs the same emotions in the people as that lovely old song. It follows then naturally for me to ask of our game's future 'pwy fydd yma 'mhen can mlynedd?' Who will inspire the songwriter in the season 2078-9? Who will sharpen the pencil of a Gren? Who will fire the kiln of a John Hughes? Who will incur the wrath of a McLean or befriend a J.B.G.?

When I first began to ponder over the question my mind went back to a dark winters night with the wind blowing up from the sea when an old man was washed ashore at Swansea Bay, hanging onto a piece of driftwood he'd fashioned crudely into a boat. His eyes were sunk deep into his skull, his skin pulled tight over his bones. He had lived on raw fish and sea birds' eggs for longer than he could remember.

The notches on his makeshift sail told of the years of drifting with ever-changing winds and tides. This ship-wrecked, weatherbeaten old man stumbled into the arms of some local fisherman.

'Tell me,' he croaked, as they wrapped him in warm blankets to rush him to Singleton Hospital, 'tell me, for I have not spoken to or seen a living person for so long. Tell me all that has happened while I have been drifting at the mercy of the sea. Has man succeeded in his attempts to put a man into space? Has the cross-channel tunnel been completed yet? Has man finally scaled Everest?'

We gladly answered his questions and then impressed on him the urgency of his condition and of the need to get him to hospital.

'One last question,' he begged. 'One last question. Tell me . . . has Charlie Faulkner retired yet?'

Charlie Faulkner, a tremendous character and a great player. One, perhaps, who has stolen a few tight heads against time and who, despite being written off a few times, has through his enthusiasm and dedication fought his way back deservedly into the Welsh side.

But what then of the future, when even Charlie will have had to call it a day. I decided the man to ask was the project engineer in the Outside-Half factory 'Dai Tolerance'.

I rang him up to arrange for a factory visit. I was met by the Works Manager who took great delight in showing me around, while explaining the many technological advances that had been made since my last visit. We went first to the Recovery Department where Outside-Halfs that had become defective were being recycled and treated. The most common fault, he explained, was malfunction of the judgement diaphragm which resulted in players kicking when in fact they should have passed. The treatment was brilliant in its conception and so simple. It required the player under test to sit in a booth where simulated match conditions were shown him on a screen complete with a sound track of crowd noises. When the film was shown he was encouraged to press a green button marked 'pass' if he saw fit, or a red button marked 'kick' should he decide otherwise. If according to the computer he chose wrongly, an electronic impulse would energize a solenoid 'S1' and a long thin stainless steel spike (situated beneath the player under test) would be driven into the region of his buttocks. The back contact on the spike would then de-energize 'S1' and the cycle would start all over again.

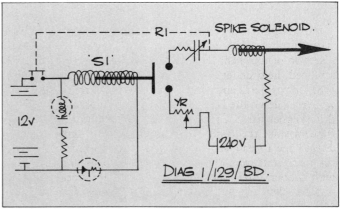

DIAG 1/129/BD.

This method had apparently been quite successful until one morning a switch stuck and the spike operated twenty-five times before the machine operator could switch it off. Needless to say, the design engineer had to be called in and

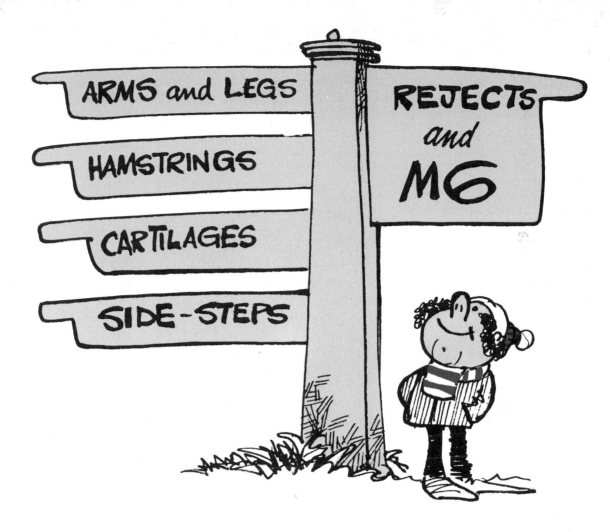

the spike (which was badly bent) replaced. The victim never fully recovered and is now playing somewhere in Surrey.

This system has, so I'm told, one other drawback. When one of the Outside-Halfs so treated (and passed by inspection) played in his first match he was instructed by his captain to kick at every opportunity because of the dreadful handling conditions. His reply was 'Only if you switch the "spike" off.'

Much impressed, we left 'Recovery' and proceeded through 'Export' and 'Arms and Legs' to a new section of the factory where the strictest security precautions were in operation.

We were interrogated and searched, then blindfolded and taken through what seemed endless twisting passageways to a section of the plant known as F.23. We were then screened, held under the strictest surveillance and searched again for cameras and tape recorders. It was only then that we were shown the latest breakthrough which according to the designer was the most exciting and revolutionary concept since the *Benny* (the swivel side-step joint). All around me I was aware of this strange high-pitched hum, all the work staff were dressed in long black-rubber suits with rubber gloves and special breathing apparatus.

It was then I saw them for the first time — *The Flair Vats*. I couldn't believe my eyes. There were these long *'nwotaes ylevol enO gninwad aesnawS em edausrep t'now enutrof A niaga nwot ym evael ton ll'I dnA em ees ot dalg eb ll'ehS.'*

N.B. In the interests of national security this section has been coded in order to comply with the official W.R.U. Secrets Act 1956. We regret any inconvenience caused to the reader. Ed.

It took me several minutes to overcome my initial shock and I was glad when the engineer suggested a cup of tea in his office. Fully recovered, we now spoke excitedly about the future of Welsh Rugby. The only thing that bothered him was the win-at-all costs attitude that had entered the game at all levels. I agreed and quoted him some lines I once wrote:

If we lose it matters not
For there the sadness ends
For defeat n'er counted as a loss
If it be the gain of friends.

I stressed to him that one of Rugby Union's finest qualities was its power to foster feelings of kinship and friendship which was far more important than winning or losing. He nodded in agreement. I was so glad to see that he felt as I did but then as I left his office I saw displayed above the door a plaque in a glass case on which was written:

When it comes for the one great scorer
To mark against your name
He'll not ask whether you won or lost
But whether you beat England.

I left his office slightly dismayed at his attitude but knowing the future of Welsh Rugby was in good hands and after visiting F.23's Flair Vats . . .

Who'll be here in a hundred years?
Pwy fydd yma 'mhen can mlynedd?

THE SEAGULLS OF LLANDUDNO

This is a song I wrote for a television 'In Concert' programme which came from Llandudno in North Wales. There had been a move in the town to cull all the seagulls eggs and burn their nests in an attempt to cut down on the number of seabirds nesting in the town. It was argued by some hoteliers that

The gulls were a nuisance
The gulls were a pest
Smash all their eggs
Destroy every nest.

They claimed that holidaymakers were tempted not to return to Llandudno because of the seagulls. Many letters were received by the local newspaper concerning the problem, arguing both for and against, the 'Seagulls of Llandudno'.

In a town called Llandudno, so the Tourist Board say
There's safe sandy beaches for the children to play
There's a prom and a pier and a café or two
And a towering headland with a breathtaking view.

CHORUS
Tooraloo, Tooralay
Come to Llandudno the Tourist Board say.

But the town has a problem, all is not well
Seagulls are nesting in every hotel
The gulls are a nuisance, complain all the guests
Smash all their eggs and destroy all their nests.

When I came last summer, I remember it well
I booked Bed and Breakfast in a four-star hotel
I asked them to wake me, a call about ten
They told me 'Don't worry, you'll be awake before then'.

An old lady told me she went there to rest
And she didn't find that the gulls were a pest
I asked 'Don't they wake you at dawn every day?'
She answered me 'Pardon, what did you say?'

'It's a job for the Council' said some in the town
'They should dress up as seagulls and shoot the birds down.'
'No! No!' said the Mayor 'You never can tell,
The chance is we'll shoot at each other as well!'

A man up from Bangor he walked in the street
When a herring gull had him from ten-thousand feet
His wife passed him paper to wipe up his brow
He said 'It's no good, love, he's miles away now.'

And now as I'm leaving the truth I will tell
I'm fond of those seagulls and I'll bid them farewell
And to those who complain and there's more than a few
Just you remember — they were here before you!

BLIMEY!!

IT CAME FROM OUTER SPACE

SWANSEA TOWN

(written by John Davis with additional lyric by Max Boyce)

*This lovely song, with its simple lyric and haunting melody,
tells of the 'hiraeth' and longing a young man has for Swansea
Town, and the happiness he feels in going home.*